AN ALIEN SKY

DEDICATION
To Jean for her love and patience

AN ALIEN SKY

THE STORY OF ONE MAN'S REMARKABLE
ADVENTURE IN BOMBER COMMAND
DURING THE SECOND WORLD WAR

ANDREW WISEMAN
WITH
SEAN FEAST

GRUB STREET • LONDON

Publisher's Note: The reader will find shaded sections of text throughout Andy Wiseman's account. These have been prepared and written by Sean Feast for clarification purposes.

Published by
Grub Street
4 Rainham Close
London
SW11 6SS

A CIP record for this title is available from the British Library

ISBN-13: 9-781-909808-25-6

Edited by Natalie Parker

Printed and bound by Finidr, Czech Republic

CONTENTS

FOREWORD

I have known Andy for some 20 years but our paths ran parallel for many years before that. We were both incarcerated in Stalag Luft III in Silesia, which has become well known as the scene of the Great Escape. There is no doubt that the creation of the tunnel was one of the most audacious exploits of the Second World War and was justified, despite the tragic consequences of the murder of the 50 officers.

Andy led a unique life. He was born in Berlin and went to school there until he was 13 years of age, during which time he tried but failed to become a member of the Hitler Youth Organisation. Coming to England, he joined the Royal Air Force which changed his name from Weizman to Wiseman and his religion from Jewish to Church of England. Shot down in 1944, he became the interpreter for the senior British officer (SBO) in Luft III and witnessed at first hand the closing stages of the war.

We experienced the same Long March in 1945 but went different ways at Spremberg, where we crowded into cattle trucks. Andy finished up at Luckenwalde, from where he was eventually liberated by the Russians.

His civilian career with the BBC was equally distinguished and after he retired we spent many hours returning to Germany with RAF personnel, re-enacting the first stage of the Long March. This brought us many new friends throughout the world.

I am delighted that he has recounted his life story and illustrated what has been such an interesting period of history, of which people should be more aware. I am very proud to have known Andy and I am sure you will find his story as fascinating as I have.

Air Commodore Charles Clarke OBE
Chairman of the Bomber Command Association
President/Chairman of the RAF ex-Prisoners of War Association

CHAPTER ONE

AN ALIEN ABROAD

I have been asked many times what was going through my mind on the night we were shot down. Was it panic? Was it fear? Was it regret for all the things I hadn't done and would now probably never get the chance to do? No, it was none of those things. I was taken over by a single, perhaps some might even think selfish thought: that I must get out. I must survive.

This survival instinct came partly from my parents, and partly from my culture. I was born, into an eclectic world, André Weizman on a perishing winter's day on January 20, 1923, in one of the coldest cities in Europe – Berlin. My father Julian was Polish by nationality and Jewish by faith; my mother, an American – a fact that would later save her life.

The local Berlin newspaper that day was full of news about French and Belgian troops who had marched into the Rhineland. It included an item that said that Berlin hotels had been ordered to refuse rooms to French or Belgian guests, that Adolf Hitler had attended a committee meeting in Munich and that butter was no longer being served in Berlin restaurants. For some strange reason, however, there was no reference to my birthday.

The First World War was still a painful memory and the humiliation of surrender and defeat even more so. Germany was obliged to repair for its folly in gold-backed marks, and by forfeiting part of the production of the Ruhr and the province of Upper Silesia. The country, under the fragile Weimar Republic, was still in a state of economic and political flux. The war had been financed by government borrowing, not savings and taxation, and was expected to be short. So when Germany lost, financial disaster was virtually guaranteed, compounded by a vengeful French military intent on ensuring the Germans paid back every penny detailed in the Treaty of Versailles. The economic free-fall peaked in 1923 with a dramatic phase of hyperinflation. At one point, a single US dollar was the equivalent of one *trillion* marks, and a barrow load of notes was only just sufficient to buy a loaf of bread or a newspaper[1].

---

1 There is a story quoted in an economic essay entitled *Paper Money* by George Goodman from the 1960s of a student at Freiburg University who ordered a cup of coffee at a café. (*cont. overleaf*)

The end to the financial chaos came almost as quickly as it had started, and the miracle of the rentenmark. Although its currency was worthless, Germany was still an ostensibly rich country, and the president of Germany's Reichsbank mortgaged the wealth of the country's farms, mines, factories and land to back a 'new' currency, the rentenmark, with one rentenmark the equivalent of one billion old marks. Although there was no 'real' value to such assets (the mortgages were fiction; the land could not be turned into cash or used abroad), a belief began to return to the German people, and with this belief came a return to what appeared at least outwardly to be a 'normal' functioning economy.

The fact that millions of people had lost their savings, their self-esteem, and needed a scapegoat was exploited by a certain German army corporal, Adolf Hitler. His fledgling National Socialist Party began its inexorable rise to power, promising the German people that their money and their honour would be restored.

Against this background and a need to forget, the Berlin socialites were determined to party. For a brief few years before the start of the global economic downturn and Hitler finally seizing power, Berlin ranked alongside Paris as Europe's party capital. New bars, restaurants and theatres began to thrive; more risqué shows and cabarets became fashionable, and huge cinemas built with full-sized symphony orchestras which provided live music to accompany silent films.

As a family we were modestly wealthy, moving in the classic middle-class circles of the time. Father was a good-looking, intelligent young man who had obtained a PhD from the university at St Petersburg and whose family had money. He ran a rather successful antiquarian bookshop, selling primarily Russian volumes, and was both well connected – particularly with those in the diplomatic service – and politically astute. My mother, Stella, was equally well connected, and his social equal, albeit that she had more time for soirées and opera than politics. She would walk into restaurants and never look at the menu; she would simply order what she wanted, much to my embarrassment.

Her father, Julius Rosenberg, was a Latvian Jew who held the concession to provide, of all things, ice cream to the Russian army. It allowed him to accumulate considerable wealth but soon after the Russian Revolution of 1917 he was obliged to leave for Berlin. The German capital was one of the

---

The price on the menu was 5,000 marks. He had two cups. When the bill came, it was for 14,000 marks. When he queried the bill, the waiter replied: "If you want to save money, and you want two cups of coffee, you should order them both at the same time."

most cosmopolitan in the world at that time and attracted all nationalities and creeds, especially those who had money. There was a very active Russian 'colony' who revelled in the high culture the city had to offer. Indeed one of my first ever memories is being taken to the Berlin opera (my father had his own box), aged five, and being so bored that I spent the entire evening counting bald heads from my elevated position.

My mother was a great traveller and it was on one of her journeys that I learned one of my first true lessons in life. I was accompanying her to Paris, and she was ahead of me as we were boarding the train. As usual she had a tremendous amount of luggage with her and was standing by the first-class compartment. I went to follow her into the carriage, only to be told in no uncertain terms that whilst she might be travelling first class, I most certainly was not and was promptly given my third-class ticket. Money, it seemed, did not grow on trees. Indeed there were other incidents from my childhood that provide the context for my character in later life. I recall once my mother asking the maid for a glass of water, and I enquired whether she would fetch me one too. My mother told me to get it myself. We lived in an enormous apartment with many rooms, and one day over luncheon my father observed, rather pointedly, that there was no salt on the table. "No," my mother said. "Where is it?" he asked. "In the kitchen," she replied, at which point my father added, "where's the kitchen?" He honestly didn't know, and I can't recall today whether he ever found it.

I was educated first at a Kindergarten and then after at the Schöneberg Staatsschule (effectively a primary school) until I was about ten or eleven. Then I gained a place at the Werner Siemens Real Gymnasium, a hugely-imposing establishment in the Schöneberg district of Berlin. The school had been founded at the turn of the century by a group of left-liberal educational reformers and was, in many respects, years ahead of its time. It encouraged freethinking and debate, and our classroom lessons were as much focused on practical life as they were the classics of Goethe. Students were invited to be involved in the organisation of the working day and local benevolence was encouraged. The school tended to be a magnet for Jewish families; in 1931, out of 382 pupils, some 212 were Jewish. They came not only from the immediate area but also much farther afield, such was its popularity. But that, of course, was before the influence of the Nazis really began to tell.

Growing up as a young Jewish boy in 1930s Germany was everything you imagine it to be only worse. As a child you recognise the injustice and the prejudice, but you are never quite sure what is behind it or why it seems to be directed specifically at you. I used to walk to the gymnasium every day, for example, with a friend of mine who was the son of the flats' janitor. Then one day he was told that he would not be walking with me anymore, because I was a Jew. His father said that he feared for his job. (After the war I went back to the flats where the janitor had lived and he recognised me straightaway and apologised for how I had been treated. His own son was at that time a prisoner of war and I helped to secure his release.)

One occasion I remember in particular: it was January 30, 1933 and we were all told to assemble in the school hall. Adolf Hitler had been appointed chancellor and we were all given the day off in celebration. Soon after, a man from the Hitler Youth (*Hitlerjugend*) came to give us a talk about the organisation and how much fun we would have by joining. The movement had been founded in 1926 as a means of indoctrinating the Nazi ideology into young boys (and later girls) and to sustain Hitler's ambitions for a Thousand Year Reich. By 1933, membership had grown to more than 100,000, but these numbers accelerated rapidly as the German leader abolished all other youth movements in preference to just the one. By 1936, some four million children had been enrolled[2]. To a small boy, the talk of the excursions and sport that we might enjoy did indeed sound exciting and I was only too anxious to join. But when my turn came, the man looked at me in disgust and literally spat out the words: "We don't need foreign f***ing Jews!" I joined the Young Socialist Youth Group instead.

As a young socialist, my principal activity was in distributing copies of the socialist newspaper, *Vorwarts* (*Forwards*), from street corners and on the trams. My father was, I think, pleased to see that I was taking an interest in politics; my mother, on the other hand, simply told me to wrap up warm. I did, however, find another way of fighting the system with nothing more or less dangerous than a whistle.

The house in which we lived on Innsbrucker Straße had a balcony that overlooked the main road. On the middle ground dividing the two highways, a *Sicherhietsdienst*[3] man would appear regularly with an enormous Alsatian dog, teaching the brute to obey his every command. The animal would sit, heel and fetch at the blowing of a dog whistle, the type that only dogs can hear. Sensing some fun, I went to the local pet store to buy an identical whistle. The next time my dog-loving Nazi appeared below me, I would hide out of sight and every so often blow my whistle, causing chaos to the

---

2   Hitler said of his German children that they must be "...as swift as a greyhound, as tough as leather, and as hard as Krupp's steel."

3   A member of the SA – the infamous 'brownshirts'.

training session. The man never did fathom why his dog was behaving so erratically.

One evening in February, the month after Hitler seized power, I was asleep in my bed when my father came into my room to wake me and told me to get dressed quickly. We were going out. It was late, at least to a boy of ten, and my father was behaving rather strangely. We headed off into the night and across the city where there was a great commotion, and crowds of people running around the streets or stopping to stare at a tremendous conflagration. The Reichstag, the rather magnificent government building, was ablaze, and a large corps of firemen was struggling to get the fire under control. I stood aghast at the flames as my father told me I was watching history. I just remember wanting to go home.

Events were steadily taking over our lives as the National Socialists began to enact the first of more than 400 legal restrictions on people of our race. Jewish doctors were suspended from Berlin's social welfare services; newly-qualified Jewish lawyers could not be admitted to the Bar; the number of Jewish students in schools and universities was limited. The biggest change came with the signing of the Nuremberg Race Laws that excluded German Jews from Reich citizenship and prohibited them from marrying or having sexual relations with persons of German or German-related blood.

To be a 'foreign Jew' at that time meant that we were not immediately impacted by the German anti-Semitic laws. It was only a matter of time, however. Jewish shops were being daubed with the yellow Star of David or had their windows painted with the word 'Juden'. Young thugs would loiter to prevent 'decent' Germans from shopping there. There was little violence – that would follow later – but the meaning was clear, and the meaning was that Jews were not welcome.

At school, certain Jewish boys were bullied, and their bullies went unpunished. Some children were ridiculed openly by their teachers; other teachers – Jewish teachers – were sacked, and our principal forcibly retired. On trains, buses and trams, German Jews had to sit on seats that were allocated to them, and nowhere else. Within the Gymnasium, the Jewish children began to leave in large numbers. By 1934, the number of Jewish pupils had dropped to only 72, and the senior school had to close for lack of students. In May 1935, the school was shut down by the Nazis, and re-opened as a vocational school for girls.

As a family we were better treated generally than German Jews but it had become clear to my father that to be a Jew of any kind in Germany was not to be recommended and so he made plans for us to leave the country while we still could. At the time we did not flee far, indeed only across the border into Poland where my father had family. This was a difficult period for me, and indeed my parents who would argue with each other continually and with tremendous passion. I was sent to the French Lyceum in Warsaw, but could not speak the language well enough and understood little of what was being taught. I was soon after sent to a Polish school, and although my command of the Polish language was not perfect, I quickly learned. Over the next two or three years living in Poland I soon became fluent in their language. We spoke Russian at home, and although I was still only a teenager I could now speak Russian and German fluently, and had conversational Polish and French. They were skills that were to help me greatly with what was to follow.

I have few memories of my time in Poland, other than at school. One day in our history class, I asked my teacher (rather naively on reflection) whether we could study something around German-Polish relations in the 20th century. He said that indeed we could, and told me to write an essay on the subject. Now my uncle's wife happened to be a teacher at another school (who for some reason didn't like me very much) and I asked her whether she would instruct her pupils to write something similar. She did, and so I had sight of some 25 or so different essays from which I could pick the best bits for my own dissertation.

I also hated Latin (what schoolboy doesn't) and had the same Latin master who had taught my father. One day in a test, I had made out a crib sheet to get me through it. I was called out in front of the class, and told to translate a passage. Unfortunately, my crib was somewhat flawed. I had inadvertently turned over two pages instead of one, so I stood there giving a translation that bore no resemblance to what was actually on the page. The other children started laughing but my teacher most certainly didn't find it funny. Indeed he was rather angry and said: "Your father's one failure is his son. What would he say to that?" I replied that since my father was paying his salary, he might not be best pleased. I was inevitably sent home, and my mother insisted that I be given extra lessons. My father was meant to help, but I discovered that he was not as good at Latin as he made out, and threatened to expose his weakness to my mother. Despite his protestations and accusations of blackmail, we agreed that the extra lessons would stop and I would keep quiet.

By the beginning of 1939, my father said that war was inevitable. We had come through the false dawns of Munich and now it looked like a global conflict was simply a matter of time. Indeed he predicted that the Germans would invade Poland in September. I am not suggesting he was a clairvoyant or a great military strategist or any such thing, but he reasoned that by the end of the summer the harvest would be in from the fields and the roads would be dry, creating ideal conditions for the German Panzers to sweep across the country.

I was by now 16 and of semi-military age, and that presented a problem. It meant that I could only leave the country with an exit permit, and the only way I could do that was if I was declared unfit for military service. My parents engineered an appendectomy, and while recovering from having my otherwise healthy appendix removed I left Poland in July 1939.

My parents, of course, were left behind. They were in the act of divorcing. It was perfectly friendly as divorces go, but they had simply decided that they didn't want to stay with one another any longer. There was a heated argument between the pair of them about me and about their future given what was happening in the rest of the world. My father had to stay, but he insisted that my mother get out of the country. My mother, who was a stubborn and determined woman, refused to leave. I remember her saying that my father always had to argue about everything, and that was one of the principal reasons she was leaving him.

Through various contacts it was arranged for me to travel to England. I wanted to fly across but my mother decreed it was too dangerous (how ironic a statement that proved to be) and so I went instead by train and by boat, and made my way to Highcliffe-on-Sea and a school called Cranemoor College. It was a strange sensation, being in a totally foreign country and once again having little or no knowledge of their language. I was greeted cordially by the headmaster, Mr Pettipher, to discover that my fees had all been paid in advance and I had nothing to worry about, at least financially.

Cranemoor College was as small as it was exclusive. There were only 20 or so students, all of us foreign nationals, and every one of us was assigned a personal mentor, in my case an Oxford undergraduate. The method of learning was much as you would teach a baby. At first it was just small words and pointing, and then over time your language and vocabulary improved. We only ever spoke English together and did not begin to look at English grammar until we could conduct a basic conversation.

Cranemoor is described in *Paton's List of Schools and Tutors* (1929) thus: 'A coaching establishment on new lines. Cranemoor is a large country house in an ideal situation on the south coast, near to the New Forest and the sea. A limited number of boys are accepted between the ages of eight and seventeen years for personal supervision over health and education under conditions of healthy home life. Preparatory section for younger boys; tutorial methods for older pupils. Special individual coaching and preparation for examinations as desired. Cranemoor affords an opportunity for the boy who has lost time through illness or otherwise to regain lost ground under congenial conditions, for the normal boy to find a new interest in learning, and for the brilliant boy to achieve further distinction. Much outdoor life. Generous, well-balanced diet with abundant vitamins, wholemeal bread and new milk. A marked improvement in general physique is observed in boys commencing residence at Cranemoor. Fourteen acres of playing fields and paddocks. Electric lighting and modern sanitation. Entire charge can be undertaken.'

It was only weeks after I arrived in the UK that my father's predictions came true, and the mighty Wehrmacht smashed through the borders of Poland. On the day that war was declared, I was standing in the headmaster's study with another boy who was German. We listened as the British Prime Minister, Neville Chamberlain, announced to an expectant nation that the Second World War had begun. Chamberlain and his ministers had sought but not received the assurances they needed, we heard, and their promise to protect Poland must now be honoured. The German boy and I shook hands; we did not know what else to do and yet in some ways the announcement and its significance needed to be acknowledged.

My school studies proceeded successfully enough and within a year I had matriculated, having passed a series of rigorous exams set by the University of London (my certificate is dated September 1940). The English exam I remember in particular: I studied Tennyson's *Charge of the Light Brigade;* Shakespeare's *Julius Caesar;* and Kenneth Grahame's *The Wind in the Willows.* I could cope with Tennyson and Shakespeare, but *The Wind in the Willows* was never going to be part of the Polish school curriculum and the concept of a toad as a central character, with all of the nuances of the story, completely passed me by. (I was none the wiser even when I re-read the book in later life.)

My parents – my mother in particular – wanted me to go to Oxford, and she made this clear to me in her letters. Academically it was certainly within reach but I, like most young men at that time, wanted to fight. I discussed it with the headmaster with whom I had developed a good understanding. Mr Pettipher, if I remember rightly, was the Liberal candidate for Bournemouth and so was both kindly and enlightened. He helped me decide to join the

Royal Air Force – a decision I especially recall as being the first that I had made without the interference of my mother. I had always liked the idea of flying, and certainly did not fancy either a life at sea (I suffered from sea sickness) or fighting both the enemy and the mud on land.

At the time I was living at the college, thanks to the benevolence of the headmaster. I had arrived in England with an allowance of sorts, but by now my funds were running low. Pettipher knew this and so retained my services to help teach history and geography to new students at a rate of £1 per week. Within that fee, I was also expected to fill a hot water bottle each night from the Aga oven and take it up to the headmaster, his wife and her mother.

It was on July 31, 1941, not long after I had turned 18 that I formerly applied to join the RAF and attended an aircrew selection board (ACSB) and was immediately placed on the reserve having been 'recommended for training as a pilot/observer'. I fully intended to become a pilot, but there were only so many aircrew the RAF could train at any one time and they did not seem in too much of a hurry to start with me.

While I awaited further instructions, quite a few things happened in my life. Having been a victim of the National Socialists' racial prejudice in Germany, I now found myself on the receiving end of new alien laws in my adopted home of Britain. There were two categories of aliens: friendly and enemy. I was, of course, in the former category but there were still restrictions in terms of when and where I could travel. There was a curfew, for example, between sunset and sunrise, and I was not allowed to journey further than five miles from my place of residence without the specific permission of the chief constable of Hampshire. I was also not allowed to own or use a camera, in case I should take photographs that could aid the enemy. One of the other things that a friendly alien was not allowed to do was to join the Home Guard; they trusted me only so far but that did not mean they would give me a rifle. I still managed to do my 'bit' however, by joining the ARP (Air Raid Precaution).

It was while I was teaching at the college that I first met Jean, the girl who would later become my wife. Jean's mother was a friend of the headmaster's wife. The Pettiphers had a son, Bill, with polio, and his treatment included long periods kept within a metal cage, and Jean would talk to him. On one particular visit, her mother had to leave early, and the headmaster promised that her daughter would be escorted home by his most reliable pupil. I didn't realise it at the time but that happened to be me.

Jean was four years older than me and very beautiful. We started seeing each other regularly but there were often practical difficulties because of my curfew. One evening, when I should have been at home, I was having supper at Jean's when the phone rang. It was the local Highcliffe police sergeant and he was looking for me. Happily I had a good relationship with the man in question, and he was calling to warn me that the superintendent from Christchurch was mounting a snap search of my digs and that I needed to get home quickly. I pedalled for all I was worth to get back in time, and just managed to clamber up the stairs, kick off my shoes and jump into bed otherwise fully clothed when the policemen arrived. The superintendent spoke to me and seemed satisfied that all was well. Then, just as he was walking out of the door he turned and said with a smile: "If you take your trousers and jacket off you may be more comfortable."

It was in early September when I at last reported to the Aircrew Reception Centre (ACRC) at St John's Wood (Lord's Cricket Ground as everyone who served in aircrew will recall), but before I did so I wrote a cheeky letter to the chief constable for permission to travel. I said that I was joining the Royal Air Force and therefore needed my travel restrictions to be lifted. The response I received was a masterpiece in bureaucracy. The actual letter has long since disappeared but I recall certain phrases that in effect said that while he was happy to grant his permission and indeed wished me luck in my endeavours, upon 'the victorious termination of hostilities the Home Office rules would be re-applied'. It seemed that my alien status was only being temporarily rescinded. They were happy for me to fight for their country but my freedom was only guaranteed whilst hostilities continued.

There was another problem too. The British government had signed a document with the Polish government in exile agreeing not to accept Polish nationals into the British armed forces (and vice versa). A Polish army lieutenant and sergeant therefore arrived at the school to arrest me for desertion. The school butler, however, forcefully instructed them to leave, and happily they did so. My father used his political connections within the British government to find a suitable 'fix'. I was told that if I were ever in difficulty and needed help, to write to Konni Zilliacus, a far-Left Labour Member of Parliament (MP). Through him he arranged an audience for me with General Sikorski, the Polish prime minister in exile and commander-in-chief of the Polish armed forces. Although I had been passed medically fit to join the RAF (the medical lasted the whole day), I was given another cursory examination and declared as 'Cat C' – unfit for active service in the Polish forces. They wanted me to join the Polish army, then in Scotland, as a clerk, but the general intervened and said that I could join the RAF if I swore an oath that I would return to Poland as soon as the war was over. I readily went along with the charade, even though at that time I had already pledged my oath of allegiance to the air force.

General Sikorski had fought with distinction in the First World War and later during the Polish-Soviet war that lasted until 1921. He held a number of government posts in the 1920s including minister of military affairs but fell out of favour and was marginalised following the coup of 1926. Requests for military command were continually denied, even after the German invasion of Poland in 1939, obliging Sikorski to escape to France where he finally attained authority over the Polish armed forces in France and soon after became the first Polish prime minister in exile. Sikorski was killed in July 1943 when the aircraft in which he was a passenger plunged into the sea immediately after taking off from Gibraltar. Sabotage has always been suspected; conspiracy theorists claim that Stalin, and possibly Churchill, wanted Sikorski dead because he was an impediment to good relations between the two allies. The general had broken off diplomatic relations with Moscow after the disclosure that Stalin had ordered the murder of hundreds of Polish prisoners of war in what is now known as the Katyn Forest massacre.

On the very first day at ACRC we were kitted out with our uniforms. While I was standing in line, I struck up a conversation with the man behind me, and when I asked him where he was from I was delighted (and somewhat surprised) to hear that he came from Warsaw. At least that is what I thought he said. Since my English was still far from perfect, I switched immediately into Polish, only for my words to be greeted with a blank stare. He did not come from Warsaw at all but rather Walsall. I am not sure who was the more embarrassed.

Having received our uniforms we were also issued with our dog tags – one red and one green; one was fireproof and the other waterproof, which did make me wonder what the war had in store for us. The dog tags featured the owner's religion and I noted that mine had been stamped with C of E (Church of England). Although I am not a religious Jew, I am a racial Jew and had seen too much persecution simply to let this pass without comment. The officer in charge explained that he could indeed issue me with a new ID, but that would mean that the machines that produced the dog tags had to be stopped and the settings changed, and all of this would take time. I asked what difference it really made, and he told me that it was only important if I was killed, so that they could ensure they afforded me the correct religious ceremony. I decided to leave it as it was.

At ACRC we lived in a block of flats – half a dozen or so of us to a room – and it was far from comfortable. There were no cooking facilities as such so for breakfast and lunch the RAF aircrew cadet menagerie was marched (the RAF had us marching everywhere) to the nearby zoo and dined in the monkey house, which seemed somehow appropriate. For supper we were given a small allowance and expected to fend for ourselves. Having had the rudiments of air force life drummed into us for the first three weeks, I was posted (on September 27) to 9 Initial Training Wing (9 ITW – part of 54 Group) in Stratford-upon-Avon. We were billeted at the Falcon hotel – again about eight or ten of us to a room – and while the Falcon may have indeed at one time enjoyed its pomp, it was a tired and weary excuse for a hotel by the time we arrived. Indeed to call it a hotel at all conjures up completely the wrong impression.

At ITW we learned some of the basics of service life, including how to clean our kit. Needless to say the concept of polishing my own boots or buttons was not something that came easily to me – it was something as a boy that had been left to the maids. But the biggest mystery was our belts that had to be whitened using 'Blanco'. A young female acquaintance, a hairdresser's assistant, suggested the answer was bleach, but not to use too much. I gave it a try but clearly my understanding of 'not too much' was different from hers, and my belt effectively disintegrated. I was put on a charge for destroying government property and given seven-days confined to camp.

Drill was of course a major component of ITW and every Sunday we were obliged to fall in for church parade (it was compulsory; there was no such thing in service life as an agnostic or atheist) and marched to the nearest Church of England church at which the order was given for the Catholics and Jews to fall out. We then marched to the nearest Catholic church and the Jews were told to fall out. For the Jews there was no synagogue, and Sunday is not a holy day; we marched to the cookhouse to peel potatoes. After that, every Sunday I varied between being C of E or Catholic – anything to get out of having to bash spuds.

Routine was important to the RAF, and routine dictated that every Wednesday we would have physical education (PE) with the typical NCO PE instructor. On one particular occasion they sent us on a cross-country run that took us into some nearby woods. Now if there is one physical exercise I dislike more than any other, it is long-distance running, so as soon as we disappeared into the woods and I was confident I could not be seen, I stopped to have a cigarette. Indeed I smoked a couple of cigarettes before our party returned and I attempted to rejoin them at a stage when it would not be obvious what I had done. Unfortunately I was somewhat out with my timing, and as I emerged I found myself near the front of the pack and ended up finishing third. The instructor was so impressed that I was selected to represent Training Command in a future event. It was another lesson learned.

One night I was on guard duty, for which we were issued with a truncheon (at this stage we did not seem to be trusted with a rifle). The officer commanding approached and I challenged him in the time-honoured fashion: "Halt – who goes there." He replied, "friend", to which I said "advance, friend, and be recognised". The OC told me he had forgotten his ID; I apologised but firmly told him that without his ID I could not let him pass. We then had the comedy exchange with the officer shouting "don't you know who I am" to which I had to admit that I did but I could still not let him pass. He demanded that I summon the corporal in charge and this is probably when I made my mistake. I told him I did not need the corporal and that I was perfectly in charge of the situation. The shouting continued, however, and then the panic began to set in and I finally let him pass. This time the officer called the corporal and told him that I was to be put on an immediate charge – for allowing an officer to pass without the proper ID. It was an early lesson into the madness of service life.

Our leisure time was spent mainly in local pubs and at occasional dances that were held in the local theatre. The authorities were not keen on us drinking and so spirits were off limits unless you were invited upstairs as a guest. I got chatting to a young girl and she asked me what I thought of the officer commanding. I told her that in all honesty I thought he was a bit of a shit, and recounted the incident of the missing ID. She laughed and invited me as her guest upstairs where she promptly strode over to the OC with me trotting dutifully behind and said: "Daddy, I'd like you to meet Andy. He's been saying some very nice things about you." I'm not sure who was the most surprised.

My first chance to fly came over the winter of 1941-1942 at 9 Elementary Flying Training School (9EFTS) at RAF Ansty which is not far from Coventry. Ansty was an unremarkable place and I have little recollection of my time there, other than my instructor. He was Greek, and totally and uncompromisingly mad. It was rumoured that he had been a fighter pilot but kicked out of his squadron for flying under a bridge. It was a rumour that we could easily believe was true, for on one occasion at least with me in the cockpit he flew so low over a steam train that I thought he was going to strike up a conversation with the engine driver!

We trained on the ubiquitous Tiger Moth, a biplane with struts and wires that looked like it belonged in a museum but which has deservedly achieved legendary fame, and each of us was given a dozen or so hours of instruction before being sent off for a first solo. Unfortunately, my instructor considered me too much of a liability to take sole responsibility for his aircraft, and as my hours continued to climb it became obvious that I was not going to make the cut. I was not a mechanically-minded young man; unlike many of my contemporaries, for example, I did not own or ride a motorbike and engines did not interest me. I honestly believe that had I had more time I could have made a competent pilot, but the RAF had their targets (even in those days) and quotas to fill, and those quotas included the need for trained observers. So it was that I found myself 're-mustered' and packed off first to Blackpool (where much of the detritus of the air force ultimately found themselves) and soon after to Brighton at the other end of the country.

In Brighton I was billeted at the Grand Hotel, even though it was nowhere near as 'grand' as it sounds. Rumour had it that the group captain in charge of our party was the hotel owner, but we were never sure. Again there was more marching, and this caused me quite some difficulty. I am not quite sure why, but I have never been able to march in step. I suppose I could if I really tried to master it but could never see the point. Unfortunately it brought me into conflict with a particular red-headed temporary corporal who, perhaps justifiably, singled me out for special attention. My contempt of the man must have been obvious for one day he shouted at me:

"Do you think you are intelligent?"
"I don't know, corporal."
"Are you more intelligent than me?"
"I don't know corporal."
"Why do you march like a pregnant duck?"
"Because you keep f***ing me about!"

My reply ensured 14 days confined to barracks (I assume it was for 'conduct unbecoming good order or discipline' which seemed to be the 'catch-all' when they wanted to punish you), which upset me because I had been due to see Jean the next day and would now have to put our plans on hold. Fortunately, one of the flight sergeant NCOs seemed to take pity on me.

He was also Jewish and had served in the First World War suspended in a balloon, spotting for the artillery. For some reason he liked me and made me a special policeman responsible for making sure the men were back in the hotel by 10p.m. In return for my night duty I was well-fed and excused morning parade.

But I soon put up another black. Not happy with goading my red-headed nemesis I took my dislike a step further. One day while marching with my colleagues, I stuck my foot out so that the NCO tripped over it. Of course all hell let loose and I was once again brought up in front of the flight lieutenant on a charge. The indictment said that Cadet Wiseman, while on active service, 'wilfully and maliciously' tripped corporal so-and-so thus causing him actual bodily harm etc. The flight lieutenant – the same officer who had already given me 14 days – asked me whether I was guilty or not guilty of the charge. I was prepared to say that it was 'wilful' but refused to plead guilty to the act being 'malicious'. The flight lieutenant asked me again, and again I gave him the same answer. Clearly a little frustrated at my filibustering, he gave me one last chance to do the right thing: I was either guilty, or not guilty. I pleaded guilty, and was given another 14 days with the term to serve concurrently. My command of the English language did not allow me to understand what he meant, but needless to say I was happy with the outcome.

The weeks dragged painfully in Brighton as the summer turned to autumn and the RAF again appeared in no rush to get me into the war. Some of our time was spent clay pigeon shooting, I assume to help us in the art of gunnery that would come later, but more likely because it gave us something to do. The tedium of service life led me into more trouble and more learning of life's lessons. I learned the meaning, for example, of the advice never to volunteer when on one occasion when asked by an NCO whether I was cold and answering in the affirmative, I found myself despatched to the nearby gas works to fill sacks with coal for heating the officers' mess. On another occasion, an NCO asked me whether I was musical. When I answered 'yes', I was despatched to help move a grand piano from the first floor to the ground floor of the officers' mess.

Despite my lack of marching ability, because of my height I was the right marker for our squad, the man around whom the whole flight is expected to formate upon instruction. On one occasion, when dangerously bored, I decided to pinch one of the horse-drawn carriages (a fiacre) that were in plentiful supply at a seaside resort just at the point that our squad was being assembled. As the NCO shouted 'markers', I appeared from around the corner and trotted past to much hilarity. Clearly, however, the NCO was not amused and I was once again on a charge for 'conduct unbecoming' etc. Of course I attempted to argue my case to the extent that there was nothing in the King's Regulations to state that I could not turn up for parade in a horse-drawn vehicle, but the RAF always wins in the end.

Not all of my time in Brighton was wasted, however. I had the good fortune while I was there to befriend a corporal who was regular RAF and who had volunteered for aircrew training. He taught me a great deal about service life (and the British people) and how you could still have fun whilst playing the game, for that is exactly what it was. I remember one piece of advice in particular: that if you are walking from A to B, always carry with you a piece of paper or clipboard, for no-one ever stops you if it looks like you might be on official business.

News reached us before Christmas that the next stage of our training was going to be overseas, and in our case South Africa. Very early on in the war the powers that be had recognised that training large quantities of airmen would be safer conducted many miles from the warzone. The risks were great enough without having the enemy to contend with. As such, training establishments were exploited in the US, Canada, South Africa and Rhodesia (now Zimbabwe) where novice pilots and observers could learn their trade in comparative safety.

From Brighton I therefore headed by train north to the Firth of Clyde, and once again found myself in trouble. I was out one evening in a pub near the docks and was nearly killed by one of the locals. I had partaken of a few scotches and he offered to buy me another. By this stage I had had more than my fill and politely declined. Unfortunately he did not take kindly to my refusal and threatened to kill me. Discretion being the better part of valour, I slipped away at the first opportunity.

There were two schools of thought when moving large numbers of troops by sea: one was to pack them, sardine tight, on to the faster former ocean liners (nearly every troop ship had once been a luxury liner) to speed singularly to their destination and rely on that speed to avoid enemy submarines; the other was for the troop ship to be part of a major convoy, and this was the tactic favoured in my case.

Being part of a major convoy was an impressive sight, ships of all shapes and sizes pitching in the swell, and it took some time for all of the vessels to assemble. We were a mixed congregation. As well as airmen there were a number of soldiers on their way to the Middle East, and a party of Wrens.

The soldiers slept below the waterline and rarely, if ever, saw the light of day. The RAF slept above them in hammocks. The officers slept up top and the Wrens were invited to dine with them. Most of the girls preferred to mix with the RAF boys, and would smuggle drinks down to us in miniature bottles containing beer, wine, gin, scotch – indeed any booze they could lay their hands on.

The journey seemed to last forever; there were constant drills for U-boats though what we would have done to defend ourselves I'm not quite sure. We had a popgun mounted aft, and every so often they would fire off a round or two to make themselves feel better. We were offered a bottle of beer on one special occasion, but other than that it was a sober ship.

We'd left Scotland, according to my service record, on December 5, 1942 and arrived in Cape Town nine days later. Having disembarked we were taken by train to 48 Air School in East London, a large and intimidating camp that featured both RAF and South African Air Force (SAAF) personnel and instructors with their distinctive uniforms. Whatever the truth of it, East London was at first a pleasure after the claustrophobic conditions on the ship, but we soon after put things into perspective. As a contemporary of mine wrote at the time:

> "East London seemed fine when we first arrived but now I am seeing things in perspective. It is about 50 years behind the times and governed by the Dutch Reformed Church. On Sunday, for example, no cinemas are open – the YMCA and the canteens do their best but that is totally inadequate."[4]

For me, apartheid was also a terrible thing; black people were barred and shunned everywhere we went. Having suffered discrimination it was something I abhorred, but there was nothing we could do about it. It was ingrained into their Afrikaans culture, their way of life, and nothing that we did or said was going to change their views. Indeed we would only create trouble by making a fuss, and the RAF was ordered to stay silent.

The first part of my training lasted about eight weeks during which time it was almost all classroom-based lectures and tests. Much of what we learned at ITW was expanded upon, and of course we were given more detailed (though still elementary) training in navigation.

---

4 From the diaries and letters of Flight Sergeant Peter Noble, 150 Squadron, killed in action December 1944.

Having successfully negotiated the first part of our course, we were next posted to 42 Air School where most of our training was in the air in twin-engined Avro Ansons that had been converted as flying classrooms.

Everything that we learned on the ground was now put into practice in the air, and not just navigation. An observer was expected not simply to 'observe', but to take away from the pilot all of those duties that a single man could not do alone. Thus it was that we were also schooled in air bombing, air gunnery, and also use of a camera for reconnaissance work. (We were the original multitaskers). In short order we learned how to recognise roads and railway lines from the air, and master the art of dead reckoning (DR) navigation.

I was rewarded for my efforts with the award of the observer's brevet – the 'flying arsehole', a name determined by the brevet's distinctive shape. As it was I believe I was one of the last observers to qualify, for soon after our duties were split into two new aircrew categories, navigator and air bomber (bomb aimer). Our whole course (there were about 25 of us – two officers and the rest sergeants) was paraded in front of the commanding officer, and our names were each called in turn. With a quick salute and a handshake, our part of the ceremony was over and we returned to the ranks with our new 'prize'. I have to admit to feeling some pride in the achievement, and news that I had myself been recommended for a commission. Our course (Course 10) celebrated in style with a slap-up dinner in a local hotel in Port Elizabeth. The date was May 7, 1943; the war still had almost exactly two more years to run.

Our return to the UK was on the *Île de France*, a former luxury liner, and while we waited to join our ship, if I remember correctly, we were billeted in huts where the permanent staff told us that the camp had been condemned in the First World War as being unfit for German prisoners of war. I also recall that the officer in charge of our course was an Indian fighter pilot who was of course banned from the pubs and cinemas in South Africa.

The *Île de France* had been built not long after the end of the First World War and was a modern wonder. We had cabins. She had been seized by the British in Singapore after the French surrendered, and pressed into service as a troop transporter. This time we were not part of a convoy; the ship could sail at more than 20 knots and so relied on her speed for safety. The plan was not foolproof, however. The journey was punctuated by frequent threats of attack and considered so serious that we were obliged to divert to Brazil and comparative safety.

This was an exciting time for us all but there were practical issues. I had little in the way of money, for example, although what I did have I spent on an engagement ring, nylons and butter for Jean. In Rio we were given shore leave and I found myself in the company of a young teenage girl whose father was a senior executive in the Bank of Brazil. They could not do enough for me and I had a marvellous time. She paid for everything; this was difficult to accept, but her father insisted and it seemed impolite to refuse.

Time soon passed and the time came for our departure once again. But before we left, the group captain asked whether any of us were prepared to stay behind. Space was needed on our ship for mothers and children to return to the UK and they needed RAF volunteers. Although it was not easy to be parted from Jean for even longer, the chance of staying in Brazil for a few more days was simply too tempting and I sacrificed myself. The decision almost proved an awkward one, for my new-found friend had amorous intentions and wanted me to marry her but I had to tell her that I was already engaged.

Despite the issue over unrequited love, we spent a lovely few days together. During the day we visited museums and libraries to soak up the culture; in the evenings it was music and dancing in the night clubs in Rio, finishing the night with a stroll along Copacabana beach. For clothes I wore her brother's shirts and trousers, for we must have been the same size (he was not there at the time). When it finally came time to go my young friend asked me if I really thought that Britain could not win the war without me. Of course I said it could not, and with that we parted. There was a job to be done, and I had my part to play in doing it.

I eventually came back to the UK in June 1943 in one of His Majesty's cruisers. The captain welcomed us on board and told us that we had a free run of the ship other than if we heard the 'woop woop' of the alarm that signalled action stations. If that was to happen, he said, we were to get below deck out of the way and let the men get on with the war.

From 7 Personnel Reception Centre (7 PRC) in Harrogate (billeted in yet another grand but rather decrepit and forlorn hotel) I was given home leave before proceeding to Wigtown (in Dumfries and Galloway in the west of Scotland) and an advanced flying unit (1 [O] AFU – the 'O' standing for observer). At Wigtown my training continued on Avro Ansons (the 'Faithful Annie') and Bristol Blenheims (once our frontline light-bomber and reconnaissance aircraft), putting into practice over the night skies of Britain the skills that I had learned in the rather more benign South African veldt. The differences were immediate and apparent. After the expanse of the bush, Britain felt rather claustrophobic, and so very 'dark'. I particularly recall my first flight in a Blenheim when I volunteered to sit next to the pilot. I did not know that the observer had to wind up the undercarriage manually, which required considerable strength and dexterity. It was exhausting. Suffice to say I never volunteered again.

At AFU I came across yet another of the RAF's more eccentric officers. Our officer commanding had some rather unusual if not to say lunatic ideas (quite literally as it happens), one of his most bizarre being to turn night into day and vice versa. That meant that we rose at 8p.m. in the evening and took our lunch at midnight. The theory was that it would help us to more easily convert to night-time operations, but in reality it simply played havoc with our natural body clocks and we spent much of the time exhausted. Logic I discovered was a quality that you did not need much of in the air force; you just did as you were told without questioning it.

At Wigtown I learned yet another valuable lesson in the British way of life. I asked the landlady in the local hostelry for a whisky but was refused. I found this all rather confusing, and wondered if it was because I was 'foreign', (the British still had their instinctive distrust of anyone who spoke in a foreign accent or who looked 'different'). One of my colleagues asked who did my laundry and whether it was the landlady. At the time it was not, but no sooner did I start using the women at the pub that I found whisky to be in plentiful supply.

I spent precisely four weeks at AFU before moving to 21 Operational Training Unit (21 OTU) at Moreton-in-Marsh arriving there as part of 64 Course on August 19, 1943. It was here that we crewed up – a wonderfully haphazard affair in that we were all told to assemble in a hangar and go find ourselves a crew. It is difficult for anyone today to understand just how simple and effective this proved to be, but it was strange to think that on looks and the very briefest of conversations alone you were trusting someone with your life.

I had only been standing around for a few minutes when I was approached by a young non-commissioned officer with 'wings' on his chest to denote he was a pilot. He was already in the company of two other men, a wireless operator and a navigator judging from their brevets. That seemed a good start. The three of them were Australian (they wore the distinctive shoulder flash) and the pilot introduced himself as Barry Casey and asked if I wanted to fly with him. I nodded and that was that. Afterwards I asked him why he picked me and he said simply that he liked the look of my face. We were now four, and spent the next ten minutes or so finding an air gunner and came across a young lad that Barry already knew so that by the end of the process we were a complete 'crew' of five.

Barry was 23 and came from Newcastle, a comparatively large town in New South Wales. He was tall, slim, blond and had blue eyes, in many ways a typically good-looking Australian. He was quiet, given the Australians' reputation, and although he liked his drink he was by no means a drinker in that sense of the word. On the ground he could be a little diffident at times, even off-hand, but in the air he was the consummate professional. The skipper: in command and good at his job, and a good friend too. He was also a good flyer.

J R 'Bob' Wallace, the navigator, was better educated than most. This was perhaps not surprising. All navigators had to be good at mathematics, and those that were good at maths tended to be the brighter boys in the schoolroom. Bob, as I was later to learn, was a very competent navigator, which was reassuring, given that the navigator was probably the most essential member of any crew. He, like Barry, was not a 'typical' Australian: he was keen, quiet and reliable. He and I also shared one thing in common: we both tended to be attracted to the same girls, which led to a little healthy competition.

Brian Richards, the wireless operator, was only 19 and had enlisted in Brisbane when he was 18. Trained in Australia, he had come to England in April 1943, and was in many ways still an innocent abroad. Brian was an incredibly shy young man who never swore and never got drunk. When later we used to go drinking as a crew, Brian often preferred to stay at base and keep his own company.

Jack Swan, our air gunner (or to be more precise the first of the air gunners who would form part of our crew) was also only 19 and very small – indeed the ideal size to squeeze into a rear turret (he was only a little over five feet six). Jack told me that he had spent his youth growing up in the small town of Glen Iris in Victoria being told by his father that Britain would inevitably be at war again and that he was never to volunteer. His father, I believe, had been in the trenches, and had no wish for his son to endure what he had himself been obliged to suffer. As soon as war came, however, he managed a complete volt face and wondered why young Jack was not already in uniform. In fairness to him, Jack was only 16 when the Germans stormed into Poland and enlisted only three months after his 18th birthday. He had only been in the UK for a handful of weeks before I met him.

I knew little or nothing of their world and they knew little or nothing of mine. They were not about to have a conversation with me about European history or culture, nor I with them about cricket or surfing, albeit I understand how clichéd that may sound on both sides of the divide. In many ways, we were all foreigners together in an alien land, miles away from home and our loved ones, with nothing in common apart from flying and the need to survive. That was what bound us all together; that indeed is what bound most if not all of the crews in Bomber Command together, especially those mixed crews of RAF and commonwealth airmen.

The Aussies were, I recall, fiercely patriotic, and torn between the desire to protect their own country and the magnetic attraction of fighting for the King and the 'old country'. Although Australians they were still British subjects. I know they felt a long way from home, and this loneliness was most obvious when they received a letter or package from their parents. (Barry's mother used to make the most wonderful fruitcakes that remarkably survived the journey in one piece.) The sense of isolation was also particularly heightened whenever news reached us of any retreats or setbacks in the war against Japan, and especially for a time when an invasion of Darwin looked possible. There was a palpable feeling among my crew that all Australians should be at home, defending their parents and family, and that Berlin could wait.

As a crew we started to do what crews did, and that inevitably involved socialising. Like every crew we had our favourite haunts, and would visit them with almost religious conviction. We had our flying pay with little to spend it on, and equally little incentive to save. With no accessible public transport, we were obliged to walk or cycle to whatever pub was locally in reach. In our case it was a public house that had resident guests, and they rather resented the often rowdy behaviour of us visiting airmen. Happily for us, the landlady had a son who was aircrew, and so turned a blind eye to our antics. She even allowed us to use the residents' lounge, often to their annoyance.

Before I came to Britain, my only exposure to alcohol had primarily been wine or fortified wine such as a port or brandy. Now I was introduced to beer, gin and tonics, and anything that would get you drunk as quickly as possible. I had no idea whether the beer was any good or not as I had no yardstick with which to measure it, but it seemed to do the trick. With the alcohol and the pub inevitably came women, and to this end Jack was a positive liability. He had a very simple, direct and effective approach: he would buy a girl three gin and tonics, and then asked her straight out if she wanted to go out with him. If she said yes then she instantly became his fiancée. It seemed to us that our intrepid Lothario appeared to have a different fiancée every other week, and even he had trouble on occasion to remember their names. (Sadly, it might rather explain why so many later came forward after we were shot down claiming to be his next of kin.)

I remember little of our time at OTU, other than that the accommodation was clean and civilised. One day seemed to blend in with the next, whether it was time in the lecture rooms ('ground instruction') or in the air on night-time cross-countries and navigational exercises. We were being prepared for war; approximately 80 hours or so of training over a ten-week period, with a new group of innocents arriving in groups of a dozen or more every fortnight.

Marching, of course, still featured prominently on the agenda, the commanding officer deciding that we had become too flabby and needed more physical exercise. The warrant officers decided one day that they would not march with mere flight sergeants, and refused to fall in. The flight sergeants in turn refused to fall in with mere sergeants and so chaos ensued. Eventually the officers gave up, and we marched smartly back to our rooms.

Flight simulation was then in its early days, and some of us observers would take time to practice 'flying' in a Link Trainer – a device that looked little more than a fairground ride but was actually very useful for teaching us the basics, with a real instrument panel and a hood that closed over your head to simulate flying at night. We also had one of the first-ever bombing simulators, an enormous contraption that was supposed to help us with successfully bombing the target but was so far removed from reality as to be virtually pointless.

Our 'real' flying was carried out in clapped-out Wellingtons. The Wellington had been one of the RAF's top-line bombers and had borne the brunt of the early bombing war alongside the Hampden and Whitleys. Now it had been superseded by the three, four-engined 'heavies': the Stirling; Halifax; and Lancaster. The remaining Wellingtons were shipped overseas for use primarily in the Middle East or relegated to a training role. It was easy to see why. In the Wellington that I flew in, you were lucky if you could climb to 12,000ft (the manufacturers claimed a service ceiling of 19,000ft), and if you coughed, the joke was that you lost 1,000ft immediately.

Training in OTU Wellingtons was nothing to laugh about, however. By modern standards, I doubt if any of the aircraft would have been allowed to fly today. Nearly every one of them went wrong at some time or other: hydraulics going u/s; oil leaks; airspeed indicator (AI) failures. What all of us dreaded was an engine cutting out, and although the Bristol Hercules that powered the Mark IIIs were generally good engines, they could not go on indefinitely. Engine failures in flight were common occurrences and accounted for a good many accidents in our time. A Wellington was a tricky enough beast in the hands of an experienced pilot or instructor, but for a

man with only two or three-hundred hours or less to his name, it could be
a death trap. Deaths were not uncommon; indeed there was one course I
heard about that lost almost a quarter of its number – and none of them
through enemy action.

A staggering 7,847 officers and aircrew were killed in training accidents in
the war. 21 OTU certainly suffered its fair share of casualties in the autumn
of 1943. Just a fortnight before Andy's arrival, Sergeant R V Carson RAAF
ordered his crew to bale out of Wellington R1508 when the starboard engine
failed and burst into flames. With the aircraft uncontrollable, all five of the
crew managed to escape before the aircraft crashed near Beaconsfield in
Buckinghamshire.

A few days later, tragedy befell the crew of Flying Officer Aubrey White
RAAF flying from the satellite airfield at Enstone. A misunderstanding
regarding the manipulation of the fuel tanks led to an engine cut and the
aircraft plunging into the ground a mile short of the runway and catching
fire. Four of the crew (all Australians) were killed, only the rear gunner
making it out in one piece.

An incident of 'friendly fire' led to the death of pilot Flight Sergeant
Fenwick Gilkeson en route for a Nickel raid over France. Intercepted by a
Mosquito nightfighter on their return, Gilkeson made a valiant attempt to
save both the aircraft and crew, and indeed three of his crew managed to don
parachutes and bale out before the aircraft crashed.

Two days after Andy's arrival, Sergeant F M Jude RAAF took off from
Moreton on a night-navigation exercise. Shortly after take-off, an engine
failed and Jude executed a near-perfect crash-landing, saving both aircraft
and crew.

The OTU managed to remain incident and accident free throughout
September but at the end of the first week of October, Wellington R1028
crashed on landing at Little Rissington, killing five and injuring the rear
gunner. The pilot, Flight Sergeant Jack Hazeldene was on final approach
when the port engine failed and the aircraft crashed into the back garden of
a pub. It was only by pure luck that nobody on the ground had been killed
also.

On November 11, another engine failure obliged the pilot of Wellington
Z9103, Flight Sergeant H C N Johnson RAAF, to ditch his aircraft into the
sea near Barnstaple. The crew all made it successfully into the dinghy and
floated ashore unharmed. Five days later, Australian pilot Flight Sergeant
Samuel Thrower is thought to have been at fault in a crash that led to his
own death and that of four of his crew. He crashed only ten minutes after

take-off, the result, it is believed of raising the flaps too quickly and losing valuable height whilst still too close to the ground.

Two further crashes happened in December, one of which proved fatal. On December 18, Warrant Officer G W Roberts became lost during a cross-country training exercise and was obliged to force-land on a golf course. Roberts and his crew emerged unscathed, but on the very last day of December – and indeed the last day of 1943 – the same crew, but this time skippered by Flying Officer Cyril Amos were not so lucky. While on a practice-bombing exercise, the aircraft flew into cloud over the Welsh mountains, and began to ice up. In attempting to find safety, Amos misjudged his height and flew into the hills, injuring himself fatally. Two other members of the crew were also killed.

Strange code words began to enter our everyday language at this time; one I particularly remember was 'bullseye'. A 'bullseye' was a night-time training operation to 'bomb' an imaginary target, and where the British defences were fully alerted to provide the necessary drama. In addition to the dangers that our own aircraft presented, there was also the risk of being intercepted by an enemy intruder, especially when coming in to land. The German Luftwaffe had perfected a technique of loitering around known RAF bomber and training airfields to catch us unawares while taking off or landing, when our attentions may be elsewhere. A further danger was collisions: on a busy night, with our returning bombers, there could be hundreds of aircraft in the same airspace at the same time; it was a miracle that more of our bombers were not lost in this way.

Towards the end of our OTU training I took part in what was known as a Nickel raid, which was the name given to a trip to drop leaflets on the local populace of northern France. What these leaflets were meant to achieve I can only guess; for my part I did not understand why we did not carry bombs. There were various practical reasons why the raids were deemed necessary: sending off comparatively large numbers of Nickel Wellingtons served to confuse the German nightfighter controllers that something bigger was in the offing, and steer vital resources away from the main attack. It also gave aircrew their first taste of what a 'real' operation may be like, and my first experience of enemy defences.

The leaflets were delivered to the aircraft in tied bundles, the idea being that we untied each bundle when over enemy territory to allow the leaflets to disperse over as wide an area as possible. Jack Swan was responsible for their dispatch, and made it clear from the outset that he had no intention of untying every bundle, and that more damage might be inflicted by dropping them in one go. He also threw out a couple of empty beer bottles for good measure.

Despite the risks and the dangers, we came through our course without serious mishap and at the end of November were posted to a heavy conversion unit (1652 HCU) to swap two engines for four, and learn the vagaries of the Handley Page Halifax – the type that we would eventually fly on operations. These heavy conversion units had been set up as dedicated training establishments to feed the ever-growing needs of Bomber Command for new, fully-trained crews. Previously, crews had been trained in conversion flights on individual squadrons, but the sheer volume of men now in demand made this impractical. Squadron commanders were similarly disinclined to surrender what precious resources they had to train novice crews, so better by far that these crews arrived fit and ready for action.

Our HCU was at Marston Moor, an enormous airfield that had opened in 1941. It was in Yorkshire, the heartland of 4 Group – an all-Halifax Group, and which had two satellite airfields Rufforth and Riccall. There were about 40 aircraft on the strength – considerably more than an operational bomber squadron – and all of dubious provenance. HCUs suffered in exactly the same way as OTUs in being given the squadron cast-offs as training aircraft. Forced landings, burst tyres on take-off, engine fires and pilot errors were all part of everyday life. The accident rate continued, deaths mounted, and we had not yet met the enemy.[5]

There was little in the way of comforts on such a large base and we slept in the obligatory Nissen hut, two crews to a hut. Despite the brave efforts of the single stove heater that was meant to keep us warm, I was almost always permanently cold. My Australian friends were stoic, but suffered much more I fear from the harshness of a British winter. Getting around the camp was a problem that could be partly overcome by owning a bicycle and cycling everywhere. The problem was that our bikes kept getting stolen. Very quickly you learned that if someone pinched your bike, you simply pinched someone else's. It was not especially gentlemanly, but by then most of my natural sense of fair play and decency had left me.

---

5 Between December 9, 1943 and January 14, 1944, there were six accidents at 1652 HCU, resulting in seven deaths and three further injuries. One of those injured was Flight Lieutenant David Fisher DFC, DFM, a very experienced pilot who had flown two tours of operations, both with 77 Squadron. He survived a forced landing that resulted from engine trouble only to go on to lose his life six months later while serving as a flight commander with 102 Squadron. Among those killed was Flight Lieutenant John Williams who had also won the DFC while flying with 77 Squadron. Experience was no guarantee of survival.

Our course lasted a little over five weeks, much of it spent in the classroom (I was never quite sure by this stage what else there was to learn). We also spent around 30 hours or so in the air (by this stage I had about 200 hours in my logbook) while Barry got to grips with his new charge and Bob further honed his navigational skills. As the bomb aimer it mattered little whether I was dropping bombs from an aircraft with two engines or four, so really our time at HCU was principally for the benefit of the pilot. We did, however, have to learn to work as a crew, and to this extent our number increased with the addition of two new members to swell our ranks. The complexity and size of a four-engined bomber made it virtually impossible for the pilot to monitor safely the gauges and performance of his aircraft for any prolonged period, and so the role of the flight engineer was created to share that responsibility with him. Being a much larger aircraft we also had more defensive firepower, and the addition of a mid-upper turret called for a further air gunner. Five now became seven.

As our flight engineer we were given Sergeant MacDonald[6] and I regret to say that I cannot remember him at all. I only know his name from checking through official records for he was with us for only a matter of days. Our new mid-upper gunner, however, I do recall, as he was another Australian: Flight Sergeant Bill Lyall. Bill, a solidly-built man who was 23 and from Canterbury, had been at 3 Bombing & Gunnery School (3 BGS) in Australia and seemed to know Jack and was pleased to be reunited. They had also, I believe, been at the same school, albeit a few years apart. Bill immediately fitted in with the rest of the crew and we were happy to have him.

With our course completed, and having been checked off by our relevant flying instructors and logbooks dutifully signed, we awaited our posting. But first we were given 14-days leave. There had been talk that we were going to be posted to the Middle East, but losses to Bomber Command over Europe had been so marked that their needs seemed greater. Almost two years of training (certainly in my case) was now coming to an end, and although we should perhaps have been scared, the principal emotion was one of excitement. We waited to be told where we were going; we were not to be disappointed.

---

6   Sergeant MacDonald seems to have flown with at least three different crews during his time on the squadron and appears to have survived his tour of operations.

CHAPTER TWO

A FOREIGN LAND

My Australian friends greeted the news of our posting to 466 Squadron at RAF Leconfield with great enthusiasm for it was a Royal Australian Air Force (RAAF) unit. Our new squadron was what was known as an Article XV squadron; Article XV allowed for the formation of distinct dominion squadrons in the RAF's Order of Battle. Australian, Canadian and New Zealand airmen trained under the Empire Training Scheme were therefore able to serve in Australian, Canadian and New Zealand squadrons, but the British retained control of all command appointments and promotions.

Formed at Driffield on October 10, 1942, the majority of 466 Squadron personnel were originally British, and their replacement was a gradual process. (Indeed it was only by the end of the war that the squadron gained a dominant Australian character.) Within two months the squadron had relocated to Leconfield in December 1942 as part of 4 Group and flew its first wartime sortie in the new year of 1943. At that stage in the war, there was a fashion for laying mines along Germany's North Sea coast (known as gardening sorties with the mines referred to as 'vegetables'), an activity that would become one of the mainstays of the squadron's activities in ensuing months.

At the end of August 1943, just as I arrived at OTU, the squadron was actually taken off operations so that its ageing Wellingtons could be replaced with the larger, heavier Handley Page Halifax, and specifically the Halifax III. Indeed I believe they were the first unit to get the new version of the bomber with its four 1,675bhp Bristol Hercules XVI engines that promised a faster cruising speed and improved performance all round.[7]

I must admit that I knew little about our new aircraft. Indeed I knew little about the mysteries of flight. We had been taught the rudimentaries at ITW, but since I had never owned or been allowed to drive a car or a motorbike, I was not especially knowledgeable about machinery. The groundcrews told us that the Halifax was sturdier than the more famous Lancaster, and could take far great punishment. We knew it could not climb as high, nor carry as much, but if she was less likely to be shot down, we were happy.

7 The HP61 Halifax III was capable of a maximum speed of 277mph at 6,000ft, and had a cruising speed of 225mph at 20,000ft. Maximum ceiling was 20,000ft, and she had a range of 1,770 miles. Empty, the aircraft weighed 38,332lbs but fully loaded it weighed nearly double (65,000lbs).

Conversion tended to be a lengthy process, the squadron only returning to frontline operations on December 1. By March 1944, operations were in full swing but there had been a number of casualties. The squadron lost five crews in January, three of those in one night – January 28/29. A further raid on Berlin on the night of February 14/15 accounted for two more of our aircraft. On a Main Force squadron such as ours, flight lieutenants were an exalted rank and squadron leaders even more so. They were invariably flight commanders, and we had lost three senior officers in as many weeks. We were one of the crews sent in to make good the numbers, and hoped we would not let anyone down.

On January 28/29 the squadron had put up 14 aircraft: one, piloted by Flight Lieutenant Frank Mack, was hit by flak and then polished off by a nightfighter. A second, flown by Pilot Officer G B Coombs, was also shot down by a nightfighter, coming down ten miles from Berlin city centre. The third, under the command of Squadron Leader Alan McCormack, was lost as a result of engine failure, possibly because of water in the fuel tanks. It could have been worse, for a fourth aircraft was obliged to crash-land at Matlaske, colliding with a hangar to avoid a party of workmen. The Halifax was, not surprisingly, written off. On the night of February 14/15, two more aircraft were lost, including one flown by Flight Lieutenant J D Cairns. Interestingly this too was as a result of engine failure, the fault lying with a malfunctioning overflow pump. Cairns and his crew survived to become prisoners of war.

Our first duty on arrival was to report to the squadron adjutant and he allocated our quarters. He was a pleasant fellow who had obviously read my personal record and knew that I had been born in Germany. He said that if I still had relatives in Berlin, he would endeavour to ensure that I was not obliged to take part in any raids on the capital. I was able to reassure him that the opportunity to bomb Berlin was one of the principal reasons I had joined the RAF. His offer, however, was an example of the British at their most endearing.

Leconfield was a permanent RAF station in the East Riding of Yorkshire that had been built in 1936. It had achieved some fame on the day that war was declared as the base from which a handful of Whitleys took off and entered enemy airspace for the first time. We were just pleased to be out of our huts and properly sheltered from the wind and rain. We were also pleased not to be miles away from the mess. We slept two crews to a room, the beds of each crew lined up against opposing walls. It was a tried and tested method favoured by Bomber Command squadrons at that time. It worked well until one or either of the crews failed to return, and we were reminded of the fragility of life in the most stark and obvious way possible.

Barry and the boys were very happy to renew old acquaintances with old friends from home or newer friends that they had made in training. It was not quite the same with me but I did not begrudge them their camaraderie. Being a new crew meant we were treated in the same way as the new boys are dealt with at school, and we realised it would be some time before we were accepted. It did not concern me unduly; we had plenty of time to become familiar with our new surroundings and fellow travellers.

Officially we were posted as a crew to 466 Squadron on March 3, 1944, but it is clear from the operations records book (ORB) that we must have been on the squadron strength a few days earlier, for on the night of March 1/2, Barry took part in the raid to Stuttgart without us. This was perfectly normal. All new captains, almost without exception, were obliged to fly with a more experienced pilot on what was known as a 'second dickey' trip. They did this to give them first-hand experience of being shot at before taking responsibility for their own crew on operations. It was a role not without risk; there are many tragic stories of pilots on their first 'second dickey' being shot down and killed before ever being able to command their own aircraft.

Stuttgart was not one of the squadron's most successful operations. Although 16 aircraft were detailed to take part (out of a total attacking force of 557), five failed to take off as a result of engine trouble or ice on their wings. A further six Halifaxes returned early: one with its heating and guns unserviceable (u/s); two with hydraulics trouble; one with its airspeed indicator broken; one through problems with ice; and the last with engine trouble. It was unusual for so many aircraft to foul up on one night, but by no means exceptional.

Only five aircraft managed to bomb the target successfully, and one of those – coincidentally – was Halifax LV837 with Barry in the second pilot's position. The pilot was Flight Sergeant Ernest Schuman[8]. The trip, Barry told us afterwards, had gone well. Barry was not prone to exaggeration or what the air force called 'line shooting', and simply told us that we had nothing to be afraid of. It was an experience, and we would cope.

For the better part of two weeks we continued training. All squadron aircrew, when not called for operations, were expected to take part in

---

8   Schuman, from Queensland, became something of a star pilot with 466 Squadron and was awarded the DFC as an acting flying officer in October 1944.

cross-country training and fighter-affiliation exercises. The latter could be particularly exciting, with Barry throwing the heavy bomber around in the skies, engines screaming, airframe straining, whilst trying to avoid a fighter who was equally determined to shoot us down – at least metaphorically. 'Bullseyes' also continued to be popular – the simulated night-time attacks in co-operation with local flak and searchlight batteries for additional realism.

While we waited our turn the squadron's war continued. On March 6, 13 aircraft successfully bombed the railway marshalling yards at Trappes, and for once the German nightfighters appeared to stay away, perhaps lured to another more tempting target. The following night, a further 13 aircraft took off to attack Le Mans with more mixed results, mainly because of the weather. One of our aircraft, it was later reported, went beneath the cloud cover but could still not identify the target accurately, and as a result the bombing was somewhat scattered.

Our own chance came on the night of March 15/16 when we saw our names on the battle order on the flight office notice board for the first time. (For some reason Sergeant MacDonald, the flight engineer who arrived with us from HCU, was not the flight engineer listed in our crew. For this particular flight we flew with a Sergeant E G 'Ted' Ashworth[9].) We had spent the previous week or so becoming acclimatised to squadron life, listening intently to the experiences of those who already had a good number of ops under their belts and many of whom, we were sure, were 'shooting a line'.

For the briefing we sat in groups at long trestle tables and as the CO and his various acolytes entered the room, we all stood as one until he had taken the platform, and the SPs (service police) had closed the doors behind us. At the main briefing there were just the three PNBs in each crew – all of us paid more for taking the same risks as our gunners, wireless ops and flight engineers. Indeed one could easily argue that their job was more dangerous, and this anomaly often annoyed me.

Pilots, navigators and air bombers comprised the three PNB categories of aircrew in four-engine bombers around which the rest of the crew was built. The other members of the crew received their own separate briefings from the respective 'leaders' – i.e. the gunners were told about latest nightfighter techniques and tactics from their gunnery leader, the wireless ops about

---

9 Ted Ashworth was an Englishman from Rochdale who had been on the squadron strength for several months. He flew with at least three different crews during his tour of operations and appears to have survived the war. For a time he was the regular flight engineer with Squadron Leader J F McMullan, but was not flying the night that McMullan was shot down and killed.

necessary frequencies and broadcasts from the signals leader and so on. The gunnery leader was Tom Drake-Brockman DFC, a very experienced second tour man who later went on to complete 64 operations before finally being rested. He had served initially with 40 Squadron in the Middle East. After the war he became a senior official with the Australian government, at one time serving as the minister for air.

The curtain that hung on the wall on the stage was drawn back by the intelligence officer (IO) with a certain amount of melodrama to reveal a huge map of northern Europe on which were pinned a series of ribbons at slightly chaotic angles to denote our route in and out of the 'target for tonight', which in this case happened to be Stuttgart. Barry and his friends had clearly not done a decent enough job a few nights earlier, and so we were being sent in again to finish what we had started.

Once again the squadron was to make available a near full contingent of 18 aircraft which, we were told, would be part of a much bigger attacking force of 863 Lancasters, Halifaxes and Mosquitoes, the latter from Pathfinder Force. The IO explained why Stuttgart was so vital to the German war effort, and the methods of target marking we should look out for. He was followed by the meteorological officer (the 'Met' man) who told us what weather conditions he thought we could expect en route, over the target, and for our return home. Our take-off time was set for 1845 hours.

Ask anyone who flew on operations during the war and they will tell you that the worst part was the waiting. We ate our mandatory (and much appreciated) pre-op meal of bacon, eggs and fried potatoes, before making our way to the crew room to collect our gear. Earlier in the day, when we knew that ops were on, we had flown a short air test to ensure our aircraft (Halifax LK793) was on the top line, and Barry signed a piece of paper with our groundcrew chief to say he was the happy owner – albeit temporarily – of some 65,000lbs or so of machinery, men and munitions for the next few hours. It had been drilled into us that aircraft were expensive items, and whether we survived or not was not really important; bringing that aircraft home was all that mattered.

An odd assortment of vehicles, mostly driven by WAAFs, took us out to dispersal where our aircraft awaited our arrival. At the beginning of the war, aircraft were parked together to make it easier and more convenient for groundcrews and aircrew alike. This peacetime ideal had been quickly shattered with the first wave of enemy air attacks that had taken out row upon row of fighters and bombers on the ground and exploded the practice for the folly it was. Now the aircraft were dispersed across a vast area of land that offered better protection from the enemy, but not so much protection from the biting wind and cold of a British winter. Climbing aboard a Halifax that had sat on its hardstand throughout the day, the first thing you noticed was the cold. Being metal, everything you touched left you with a burning cold sensation, and so you kept your gloves on for much of the time. I wore gauntlets, but had two pairs of 'inners' beneath them so that I could operate the computer and bomb release.

The first of our aircraft got off the ground at 18.43. A steady stream of Halifaxes then followed at intervals of approximately two minutes, including our CO, Wing Commander Dudley Forsyth DFC[10]. Our own turn came at 19.10, and we were the last but one to leave. For take-off we had developed an established routine. I would sit next to Barry at the controls, and as he put his right hand on the throttle levers to increase boost for take-off, I would place my left hand behind his so that the levers did not slip and lose power at the critical moment (take-off and landings were – and still are – the most potentially dangerous moments of any flight). As soon as we were airborne, it was then also my responsibility to confirm that the wheels had safely retracted, and then there was little for me to do except keep watch.

Our flight out to the target was a long slog in patchy cloud of nearly four hours over France to the edge of the Swiss frontier, before turning north-east to attack Stuttgart. When we were about 30-minutes flying time from the city, I clambered down into the nose to get myself ready for the attack. Stuttgart was not a happy city, and the German defenders clearly took exception to our being there. Flak began bursting all around us, mainly 88mm heavy artillery with the occasional larger calibre weapons thrown in for good measure. As high as we flew, the German shells could reach higher. It took a heavy shell about 12 seconds to reach 20,000ft, and if you heard it explode then it was too close for comfort. An 88mm shell, however, needed to be within 30 feet to be dangerous but, we were told, we would be comparatively safe if we stayed within the stream.

As we carried on to the target, I could see the occasional arc of tracer fire sparkling in the dark as a German nightfighter attacked one of the stream and/or one of our own gunners answered back, pretty little baubles of light

<hr />

10 'Lee' Forsyth was a regular air force officer, trained at Point Cook, who had earlier commanded 25 Squadron (1941-42) and served as senior air staff officer HQ Western Area (1942-43). He had been appointed OC of 466 Squadron in September 1943. He later became station commander at RAF Driffield as a group captain.

in an otherwise blackened sky. Indeed there was a great deal of fighter activity, and it came as no surprise later to learn that we lost nearly 40 of our number that night. Lying on my stomach, full length, surrounded by a clear Perspex canopy and comparatively thin metal was not my idea of fun, and I felt rather exposed to it all. But fear, concentration and training are a powerful triumvirate, and my thoughts were of nothing other than to get the job done and get home. I had an undeniably good view of proceedings.

For the bombing run, the air bomber effectively 'flew' the aircraft; the pilot did exactly as he was told through a series of instructions that I gave to him over the intercom while I peered ahead and tried to pick out the Pathfinder markers. The Pathfinders flew ahead of us to identify the target and mark the aiming point with either red or green flares (known as target indicators). A 'master bomber' would then instruct us journeymen 'main force' crews where to aim our bombs, whether directly at a particular coloured smoke, or with an undershoot or overshoot, depending on where the indicators had fallen.

With these instructions, I would then issue my own orders by calling out 'left left', 'right' and 'steady' to guide the aircraft through the bombsight until the cross hairs aligned with the aiming point. (I used to say 'left left' very quickly, and then elongate the word 'right' as there was so much noise in the aircraft I wanted to be properly understood.) I armed the bombs and selected the bomb release sequence using a magic box mounted to my right. I could release the bombs individually or in salvo, but always in such a way that the balance of the aircraft was maintained so that there were no sudden surprises. Then and only then would I call out 'bombs gone' and for the bomb doors to be closed. With the aircraft lightened of its load, Barry would open up the taps, stick the nose down slightly to build up speed as quickly as possible to get out of the target area and head for home on a course given to him by the navigator. While all this was going on, the flight engineer would be keeping a watchful eye on the performance of each of the four engines on a dedicated instrument panel, and making various calculations about fuel consumption.

Of course, as I was to discover, the theory did not always quite match the practice. Aligning the bombsight to the target was not a simple affair, and throughout the bombing run we could find ourselves under attack from flak, fighters or searchlights. Searchlights played havoc with your night vision, and you quickly learned not to look at them directly. It was a lovely idea to think that we could fly straight and level in the target area for long enough to achieve total accuracy, but it was not always possible or indeed desirable. Jack Swan, our rear gunner, made it perfectly clear to me from the outset that if I messed up the first run, we were never to go around again, on pain of death. Mine of course. As it happens we never did.

On that particular night, it all so very nearly ended in disaster. We were at 20,000ft, our maximum ceiling, having gained altitude for our bombing run, and I was just getting comfortable when Jack sensed and saw a cannon shell come screaming towards us from dead astern. He did not immediately see the aircraft that had fired it. Jack called for the skipper to 'corkscrew'[11], a violent manoeuvre that threw the bomber into an elongated spiral to avoid any further onslaught. Barry thrust the aircraft into a diving turn, the engines screaming; at the same time Jack opened fire, but was no doubt horrified to discover that only one of his four Browning .303s was working, the other three had frozen. Bill Lyall, who had seen the tracer pass no more than six inches below him, also pressed the triggers in the mid-upper turret, but not one of his guns responded.

Instead of eight guns in the two turrets to defend us, we now only had the one. Jack identified the fighter as a single-engined Messerschmitt Bf 109, an aircraft more suited to daylight operations but pressed into service as a free-ranging (so-called 'wild boar') nightfighter. He watched it as it flashed beneath us and then was gone, the skipper's evasive tactics having the desired effect.

Now we were in trouble. The attack had lasted only a second or two but in that time the hydraulics had been shot away, leaving us without essential power, the flaps on the port wing had been hit and the bomb doors pitted. The Elsan toilet – an important if rather revoltingly chemical 'convenience' on long-distance trips – had also been shot away for good measure. Another shell, we would discover later, had only narrowly missed one of the petrol tanks.

Barry went on to the intercom to check nobody was hurt, and asked Bob for a course to the target. Meanwhile the flight engineer, Ted Ashworth, reported smoke billowing out of the bomb bay and feared that the incendiaries may have caught fire. He grabbed a fire extinguisher but found that although there was plenty of smoke, for once there *was* smoke without fire.

---

11 A corkscrew was used against fighter-attack and consisted of an initial diving and climbing turn in the same direction, followed by climbing and diving turns to produce a corkscrew effect. The manoeuvre had the advantage of giving a constantly changing deflection shot that was known to the gunners but not the fighter pilot. In practice, it was unusual for the sequence of a corkscrew to be completed before the fighter was either shot down or, more likely, the attack broken off. Often the initial dive and climb was sufficient to achieve one or either of these results, if properly executed. But it was not always successful.

We continued to the target and then ran into our second piece of bad luck, a very heavy burst of flak. I was very fortunate not to have been in the bomb aimer's position at that moment, for a piece of shrapnel carved through the nose and destroyed my bomb sight. Another fragment hit our mid-upper in the leg, but caused only a minor scratch.

This left me in a bit of a predicament: how to bomb the target. With necessity proving the mother of invention, I simply aimed my bombs by sighting the target along my thumb and index finger, pressed the 'tit' on the bomb release and chanced to luck. I called for Barry to close the bomb doors but with our hydraulics badly damaged they would not budge, and we were forced to start the homeward journey with our bomb doors still open.

The effect on the aircraft was considerable. Aeroplanes are built to be streamlined for maximum flying speed and fuel efficiency, and now we had neither. The drag was such that our speed was considerably reduced, and the flight engineer anxiously watched our petrol consumption. We were halfway home and confident that we would reach base when a third piece of bad luck hit us: the port undercarriage fell down, now taking our flying speed to only just above stalling.

For our own efforts, the ORB simply states:

Primary attacked from 21,000ft at 23.17 hours. Heading 020M. Bombed Red/Green TIs. 6/10ths Cloud tops 15,000ft. Visibility very good. Landed at Winthorpe.

Of the 18 aircraft from the squadron detailed for the attack, 17 actually took off and one returned early after the air bomber fell ill. Fourteen of us managed to bomb the primary target and eight aircraft, including our own, landed away from base at Winthorpe[12], Ford and Tangmere, nearly all with some kind of damage. When the groundcrew checked our tanks upon arrival, it was found that we only had sufficient petrol for another five minutes of flying.

And so our first op was over. We had made it. Just. Barry pulled off an excellent landing in the circumstances using emergency air to lower the starboard undercarriage, operate the brakes and what remained of our flaps. After being preliminary debriefed, we were found temporary accommodation and as I lay on a bed in strange surroundings in the early hours of the morning and attempted to sleep, my mind was a mixture of emotions from fear to relief. It had been a lucky escape, but the crew had performed well.

---

12   Winthorpe was an RAF base in Nottinghamshire, home to a conversion unit. It is today the site of the Newark Air Museum.

We all learned to cope in our own ways. Some of the men were married; some had children. Every one of us was different and had his own reasons to live. We accepted that, for the duration, we had a role, and we would endeavour to fulfil that role to the best of our abilities. For my part, and with the exception of my own crew, I tended to ignore the others around me; it was important not to feel any emotional attachments. We were there to fly, find the target, and drop our bombs on the enemy. Nothing else mattered or counted.

We returned to Leconfield by train, carrying our precious parachutes and Mae Wests as hand luggage. We looked a funny sight, sat amongst the afternoon commuters. While the squadron operated two nights later to Frankfurt, our services were not required. Perhaps it was a good thing for we lost three aircraft. We lost another on the night of March 24/25 on the infamous 'night of the strong winds' – a raid on Berlin in which Bomber Command lost 72 aircraft in all, the majority because they were blown off track and into the flak belts that defended the approaches to the city and beyond. On the face of it, perhaps, we were lucky.

Our names were on the battle order for an attack on Essen, planned for the night of March 26/27. We were allocated Halifax IV919 'O' Orange. For this, our second trip, we had a different flight engineer yet again, Sergeant Abbott Camp, an older man with considerable experience, but even he could do nothing to prevent the freak accident that obliged us to return early. About an hour or so into our trip, Jack started complaining that something was wrong with his electrically-heated suit. This was an ingenious if somewhat bulky device that was intended to protect the gunners against the extreme cold that they could sometimes face in the extremities of the aircraft. Indeed there were many stories of rear gunners, exposed to the elements, returning with icicles hanging off their oxygen masks where the spittle had frozen, and even cases of frostbite.

Jack had no sooner made his discomfort known to the skipper when the suit short-circuited, sending a shooting pain up Jack's left arm causing him to be paralysed. With our rear gunner incapacitated, we had little choice but to abandon the operation, and I jettisoned our bomb load over the sea on Barry's instructions and we headed for home. Jack was treated after we landed and was soon back on his feet, but it was one of the more bizarre incidents that occurred to us or indeed any crew that I heard of at the time or since.

Our sortie had lasted less than two hours, but rather than go to bed (sleep would not have come easily if we had tried) we waited up to greet the returning crews. Sixteen had taken off but in the event only 14 reached and bombed the target. Happily, all of them made it home but not without a little excitement along the way.

For every raid where we lost one or two aircraft in a single night, and Bomber Command may have lost 50 or 60, it could always have been worse. Bomber crews were under the constant strain and fear of attack on every target, right up until the very last days of the war. Many aircraft returned damaged, and some aircraft and airmen never flew again. The 'cost' to Bomber Command should never simply be measured in the official totals of aircraft shot down on a particular raid; the price it paid was always far greater than the record books suggest.

We had more bad luck on our next operation, although given what transpired I think we may have considered ourselves fortunate. It was, in theory, a stand-down period as the moon was full and conditions stacked too much in favour of the enemy. This did not prevent the planners, however, from deciding that there was sufficient cloud cover to mount a raid on Nuremberg, a city at the very heart of National Socialism. It was to be yet another large-scale raid comprising almost 800 aircraft including 17 from our own squadron. In the event, 16 managed to get off the ground of which one returned early because the navigator fell ill, one because the heating system failed, one because the rear gunner passed out through lack of oxygen, and one because of a complete cut out of the starboard inner engine.

This latter aircraft was our own. One minute, the four engines in 'O' Orange were singing along happily; the next, the starboard inner packed up without any warning. The calm voice of the flight engineer came on the intercom to say that we were leaking fuel. This left us in a bit of a predicament – a predicament that became worse when we lost a second engine, the port inner. There was a dreadful thing in the RAF at that time called 'lack of moral fibre' abbreviated simply to LMF. In technical terms, it was when a man had forfeited his commanding officer's confidence. Put more simply, it meant he was a coward – at least in the eyes of the service. No-one that I knew ever wanted to be thought of as having LMF. Even the faintest whiff of cowardice could severely impact morale, and the officers knew it. Of course there were incidents of men who could not cope with the strain of operations, but this was often because they had suffered a severe trauma, and today would have been treated for post-traumatic stress disorder. But in 1944, PTSD did not exist – at least not officially, and certainly not in the RAF. (For my own part I had no fear of dying. Perhaps that is not quite true; yes I feared being killed, and the pain of being mortally wounded, but I feared being blinded or maimed much more.)

Crews in aircraft that returned early were almost automatically under suspicion. At best we might be considered jinxed, but that was vastly preferable to being considered yellow. Was it right to fly on to the target with three engines or return home? It was perfectly possible to fly a Halifax on two engines, although maintaining height was a problem, and the two good engines had to make up for the power lost in the others. This therefore increased their likelihood of failure, and impacted our fuel consumption, so our margin of safety was being steadily eroded. It took a strong captain to decide to return early; there was always the risk that the fault would be rectified immediately, and then we were expected to set off and catch up with the stream, placing us in arguably even greater danger. A greater worry, however, was that no fault would be found at all, and so we would be expected to account for our actions.

As it happens, after our return our Halifax was taken out of service for some time, so the damage to the engines was clearly serious. Barry pulled off an excellent landing with the two engines feathered (i.e. the leading edge of the blades turned into the wind so as to reduce drag) and not a hint of suspicion was aimed in our direction. For our own confidence, however, we wanted to get back on ops as quickly as possible, but for a week or more we had to wait out turn. The raid on Nuremberg was an unmitigated disaster, with 95 bombers being lost and scores of others returning with damaged aircraft and crews that would never fly again. Miraculously, we were one of the few squadrons to have had a comparatively quiet night, but still we were stood down while the various bomber groups licked their wounds and prepared once more for battle. I went on leave, and Jean said that I talked all night. Fortunately she was a good and patient listener.

During these periods of relative inactivity, and apart from the occasional cross-country or bombing exercise, time was often our own. Beer runs into nearby Beverley were the usual order of the day, and we were lucky in that respect to own a car between us as our own private vehicle. The car ran on aviation fuel, as I believe most cars of that vintage did, and we did not worry about parochial matters such as registration plates, numbers or insurance. We were careful, however, to keep the car out of sight from any senior officers; we were rebels, but we were not stupid.

That's not to say, however, that we did not occasionally find ourselves in daft situations. On one particular pub crawl, we were pulled over by a policeman for having a faulty headlight. He asked me, as the driver, for our registration documents. We had decided, as a crew, that the car was too expensive to insure and register and so I had to think on my feet. I said that I did not have them because we were at that very moment on our way to Hull to get the car properly registered. Whether he believed us or not, we were allowed to go on our way. A day or two later and we were stopped by the same policeman who again asked us for proof of registration. I said that at our last attempt the car got a flat tyre so we had not made it to the town hall. Now we were on our way to get it done: "Not on a Sunday you're not," came the reply and he promptly wrote me out a ticket.

The war was progressing well for the Allies, notwithstanding the occasional hiccup. At a senior level, Bomber Command was put temporarily at the disposal of the supreme allied commander to support the imminent invasion of Europe. Bombing of German cities and industrial centres was now to take second place to the so-called 'Transportation Plan' – knocking out critical road and rail infrastructure to cause chaos behind enemy lines, and disrupt the quantity of men and armour that could be transported to the front. On the positive side, trips to France were of far less endurance, although we carried more bombs as we needed less fuel. There was even talk of these trips only counting as one third of an op, because they were considered less dangerous. That proved to be ironic for a good many 466 Squadron crews, ours included.

Our first chance at one of these 'easy' targets was when 15 of us were ordered to attack Villeneuve-St-Georges near Paris. That night, April 9/10, Bomber Command's forces were split across two targets, Villeneuve-St-Georges and Lille. Lille was a disaster, at least for the local French inhabitants when the bombs fell wide of the mark and into a residential area. More than 450 French men, women and children were killed. Our attack was rather more successful; at least we did not kill quite so many civilians. For once, all 15 of our aircraft got away on time and reached the target. It was a two–and-a-half hour trip to Paris from Yorkshire in our new aircraft, LV956 'R' Robert, and we arrived in excellent visibility, the railway lines and the sheds in the marshalling yards easy to discern. There was little by way of any opposition and the flak was only light and ineffective. The ground markers could be clearly seen and I had no problem in toggling our bombs away on the primary target. We landed back at Leconfield at exactly 0300 hours, a full hour after the first of our number returned[13]. Buoyed by our success, we

---

13 One Lancaster from 460 Squadron, which was also taking part in the attack, reported no less than four encounters with enemy fighters on the raid, as well as seeing many more fighters of all types. The squadron gunnery leader was said to be inclined to treat the encounters 'somewhat warily' due to the

were pleased to see our names on the battle order for the next operation to attack railway marshalling yards at Tergnier. This was to be an all 4 Group affair, with the target marked by Mosquitoes of 8 Group. Bomb load was a mix of 1,000lb and 500lb medium capacity (MC) bombs designed to cause maximum destruction. The raid again went well. We reached the target in a little under three hours and I set about busying myself in the bomb aimer's position. Weather conditions were again in our favour and we attacked at around 10,000ft, seeing our bombs fall clearly on what we took to be the target. It was a little difficult, I recall, because the ground markers were scattered to the south of the aiming point.

Flak was only light and mercifully there were no searchlights to contend with. The flak and searchlights worked together. The searchlights were more often than not radar-controlled, and probed the night sky, often above the bomber stream. The objective was to make individual bombers take evasive action and dive, forcing them as low as possible, where the flak was more accurate. It was clear very soon that there were a good many fighters about and Jack and Bill scanned the skies for anything out of the ordinary, occasionally calling out as they saw one of our bombers in flames. Thankfully we were not troubled ourselves but soon after we landed we learned that two of our crews were missing. It was an unhappy way to celebrate Barry's birthday.

With three operations now successfully completed, we were beginning to find our rhythm. We flew a bombing exercise on the 13th and a cross-country the next day, and there was certainly no concern when we were again on the battle order for the night of April 18/19. The battle order listed our crew as follows:

Pilot	Flight Sergeant Casey RAAF
Navigator	Flight Sergeant Wallace RAAF
Air bomber	Sergeant Weizman
W/op	Flight Sergeant Richards RAAF
Mug	Flight Sergeant Lyall RAAF
R/g	Flight Sergeant Swan RAAF
Flight engineer	Sergeant Camp

We were again allocated one of the newer aircraft, 'R' Robert[14].

There were 15 squadron aircraft called and there was nothing untoward

crew's inexperience, especially since in every case the reported fighter did not open fire. He indicated he would watch their future operations with great interest.

14 LV 956 was one of a batch of 225 aircraft built between January and March 1944.

throughout the day that foretold what was to come. Unusually we did not fly an air test but neither were any snags reported. The aircraft was bombed up with the usual mix of 1,000 and 500lbs designed to explode on impact, and the combined bomb and fuel load indicated a short trip – subsequently confirmed at the briefing. We were to go back and finish the job at Tergnier. There was relief all round. We had been there before and knew what to expect. To all intents and purpose, this should be another easy one. What the Americans were calling 'a milk run'. It was certainly preferable to a long slog to Berlin, or the fierce defences of the targets in the Ruhr – the much-feared 'Happy Valley'.

The IO outlined the method of attack that was to be mixed Newhaven and Oboe groundmarking. (Newhaven was the codeword for an attack where the target was identified 'blind' using the H2S radar that 'mapped' an image of the ground below on a cathode ray screen. Newhaven and Oboe – an extremely accurate blind-bombing device – were used in conditions where the target could not be identified accurately by visual means.) Zero hour was 23.30, and the attack was scheduled to last 12 minutes – such was the deadly efficiency of our bomber streams at this stage of the war.

We ate our pre-op meal in comparative silence, the WAAFs checking our names discretely against a list of those on operations. The usual jokes were exchanged without much humour until it was time to change. Our kit – flying boots, jackets and helmets – were personal items kept in named lockers. Parachutes, harnesses and Mae Wests were drawn from the parachute section; above the counter ran the legend: 'every parachute has been personally tested by the duty sergeant; in case of failure, please report to him immediately.'

We were driven out to our dispersal early, a feature of operations that I never properly understood for it just seemed to prolong the wait. While we waited the CO, Wing Commander Forsyth, drove over to wish us well. He did this before every operation and it was generally appreciated. Forsyth had his faults; having commanded a training unit he tried to run an operational squadron in the same way and it didn't always work. There was always a rule, for example, that you did not talk on the radio unless and until it was absolutely necessary. It was distracting and potentially dangerous. The Australians, however, often did as they pleased and one night coming home from a raid a number of the crews were chattering away while they waited their turn to land. It was a way of letting off steam. Forsyth came onto the radio himself to tell the boys to keep quiet:

"I will have no chatter in the circuit," he said, rather pompously.

"Oh f**k off!" came the reply.

"Who said that?"

'Not f***ing me sir," came the response from a dozen voices, accompanied by much laughter.

But to his credit, Forsyth was not one to shirk flying. As he and the rest of the crew exchanged pleasantries, Forsyth noted that I seemed to be in a strange mood and asked me what was wrong. Jean had knitted me a golly, and I used to take it with me as a good luck token. By mistake I had left it in my locker, and in my haste to don my flying gear had forgotten to bring it with me. The anxiety must have shown in my face. Without hesitating, Forsyth spun the wheel of his jeep and raced away, returning a few minutes later with my talisman. Now at last we could get on with the war. (Long after the war I spoke to Jean about this incident. I felt that given we were shot down, the golly did not seem to bring me much luck. She pointed out, however, that I had survived, so perhaps there was something in it after all.)

We were away at 21.16, the four engines roaring as we sped along the runway and I kept my hands behind Barry's in the routine fashion until we left the ground. Then it was a quick glance to check that the undercarriage was fully up and then settle down for the two-and-a-half hour trip to the target. As we crossed the enemy coast, we started to climb through the cloudless sky to our bombing height of around 14,000ft. The weather over the target was clear, save for a little ground haze, and I listened to the instructions of the master bomber telling us to ignore one group of target indicators that had fallen to the west and instead to bomb a cluster of TIs to the starboard. I guided Barry onto the target without difficulty, pressed the 'tit' to release our cargo, and then called for the bomb doors to be closed. Bob Wallace, our navigator, gave Barry a course to steer for Leconfield and we set off for home.

So far the raid had gone completely according to plan. With luck and a fair wind, we should reach friendly territory within the hour and be home in just over two. Unburdened of its load, the Halifax was much lighter and faster, but we did not relax. The gunners maintained their vigilance, constantly sweeping the skies for any hint of something unusual, a shadow where it shouldn't be; a disturbance in the night.

My task completed, I reversed out of the bomb aimer's position to come and sit by the pilot and provide an extra pair of hands and eyes to assist as required. We all had our search patterns. The flight was going well. Barry had taken the aircraft up to about 17,000ft where it was safer, or at least we were out of range of the lighter flak. We had about 15 minutes to go before crossing the coast. Then it happened.

Suddenly there was a bang, a series of loud explosions as cannon shells from an unseen nightfighter tore through the cockpit and exploded, killing Barry instantly. He can't have known a thing about it. Then there was smoke, the smell of burning, and confusion. There had been no warning from the gunners. No return fire. Perhaps their guns were frozen again. Perhaps they had simply not seen it. Perhaps they were already dead. All I was aware of were the sights and sounds of an aircraft mortally wounded.

There was nothing on the intercom. No instructions. No screams. But then the intercom was dead. Shot away. And there was fire. Within moments, the cockpit was ablaze, a mass of reddish white flames and smoke. Bob pulled back the blackout curtain and started to go aft, getting as far as the steps that led to the rear of the aircraft when he came across the wireless op, Brian Richards, putting on his 'chute.

Because of the limited space in our aircraft, our parachutes were effectively in two parts. Part one was the harness, which we wore about us for the whole flight. Part two was the actual parachute pack itself, which you had to recover and clip on to the harness if you needed to escape. Only the pilot differed; he wore a seat-type parachute that was permanently attached, a tacit acknowledgement that if hit and obliged to leave the controls he would not have a moment to spare.

Bob made for the nose and the escape hatch and instinctively I followed. I have been asked many times what was going through my mind during all this chaos. It wasn't panic. It was a single thought. That I must get out. Bob opened the escape hatch with some difficulty – it was jammed – but eventually it broke free after he jumped on it and he jettisoned the hatch cover through the hatchway. Without any hesitation Bob dropped out into the night sky, with Brian and me behind him. I sat on the door with my legs dangling outside and followed. My mind was completely clear.

By now we were down to about 12,000ft, and the aircraft was in its death spiral, steadily corkscrewing involuntarily to starboard. It then began a shallow dive to earth. I counted to eight, as we had been taught, so that I was well clear of the aircraft before my 'chute deployed, and avoided the risk of the parachute being entangled in the tailplane as it passed over my head. Then I pulled the D-ring and after the briefest of moments my descent was arrested as the 'chute opened above me and I began to swing beneath its canopy.

All around me were the sounds of war, and I could clearly see our aircraft, on fire, prescribing an enormous blazing arc in the night sky. Apart from Bob, I could not know if any of the others in the crew had made it out. But at that moment it was enough to worry about myself and my own situation.

I could make out little of what lay below me as I fell to earth, but just when I thought I had got away with it there was a thump and a clatter, and sharp branches began scratching at my face and my body before snapping against my weight and momentum. I had landed in a field, or to be more precise, the only tree in the middle of that field.

The fighter was flown by Martin Drewes, the commanding officer of III/NJG1, for his 21st victory. He claimed a Halifax flying at a height of 5,000 metres, 30 kilometres north east of Rouen, at 0001 hours. He claimed another Halifax ten minutes later. The former was confirmed as being Halifax LV956 of 466 Squadron. Drewes had joined the German army in 1937, initially with the 6th Panzer Regiment to gain his commission. He transferred to the Luftwaffe on September 1, 1939 and spent eight months at pilot training school in Werder-Havel, attaining his flying licence in April 1940. He progressed to an advance flying training unit (the 'C' School) flying Junkers 52s, Heinkel IIIs and Dornier 17s before being posted to a 'Zerstörer' ('destroyer') school at Schleissheim in October. He joined his first operational unit, II/ZG76 (the second Gruppe of the 76th Zerstörer Geschwader) in February 1941, flying the Messerschmitt Bf 110 from its base in Jever. Posted to the Balkans in May, he flew operations over Iraq, and by the time he returned to the European campaign he had scored just the one victory. Retrained as a nightfighter pilot, Drewes found his métier, joining the sixth Staffel of ZG76 which was re-designated 9/NJG3. He took part in the defence of the three German capital ships during the famous 'Channel Dash', and the defence of the *Tirpitz* in Norway. He took command of 7./NJG3 testing the new 'Wurzburg' radar, before moving to IV/NJG1 and then II/NJG1 as its commanding officer. In February 1944 he became Kommandeur of III/NJG1 and was promoted Hauptmann. Drewes was thereafter in the thick of the nightfighting war and was awarded Germany's highest honour, the Ritterkreuz (Knight's Cross) in July, his score having reached 48. Promoted Major, his final victory came on the night of March 3/5, 1945, after which he was awarded the Oak Leaves to his Knight's Cross. By the war's end he had flown 235 operations and shot down 52 aircraft, all but two of which were four-engined bombers.

Happily, save for a slightly twisted ankle and a few bumps and bruises, I was otherwise in one piece, and again my instinct took over. We had of course received various lectures and instruction from the good people at MI9 about escape and evasion[15], and what to do if shot down over enemy territory, and some of those lectures had been given by those who had themselves escaped and made it home. We had even been obliged to take part in an exercise where we were dumped in the countryside, miles from home, and instructed to make it back to base without being caught by parties of Home Guard who were out searching for us. The exercise had descended into farce when one of our number had stolen a steam engine. Apparently, stealing cars, horses or mules was perfectly acceptable, but a railway engine was going too far. The poor man was court-martialled for his pains.

We had been told in these lectures first to get rid of our parachute and Mae West life preserver. We had also been told that whatever we did, we must try to avoid human contact, even though everything in our psychology would fight against it. We were instructed to lie up during the day, and only travel at night. As it was still dark, and I reckoned that the Germans would soon be out looking for survivors, I had better put as much distance between myself and the crashed bomber as I could. I began to wander, with no real idea of where I was heading, but it was vaguely in the direction of a farmhouse. As I got nearer, I could clearly see a well, and it seemed to be the ideal solution to hiding my gear. Having quickly removed my harness, parachute and life vest, I threw them into the well and out of sight – at least for the time being (it did not cross my mind that my life preserver would float). Just before I did so, however, I cut a small piece from the parachute silk as a memento.

My moment's reverie was interrupted by the sound of barking dogs, and I decided to move on. Despite what we had been told, the need for human contact was very great indeed and I approached two further farmhouses to seek help. On both occasions I was told in language that was clear in its meaning if not its dialect that I was to go away and so continued walking. By now it was beginning to get light, and I needed somewhere to hole up. There was a forest close by and so I hid myself deep within it. Lighting a fire was obviously out of the question, but I had my escape kit and so munched on a Horlicks tablet and a small piece of chocolate to keep me going. It wasn't much but it was all that I had, and it was certainly better than nothing.

Sleep did not come easily if at all. The adrenaline still pumping through my veins combined with the trauma of the last few hours and the cold of the

15 One of the principal lecturers was Flight Lieutenant Eric Williams, one of the three prisoners to make a home run after the famous Wooden Horse escape from Stalag Luft III.

night prevented me from getting much rest, and I was keen to move on. I decided to try another farm and having spied the lay of the land approached with caution. Once again there was barking (dogs seemed to be everywhere in France) but I was too tired to let them bother me. It was now early morning, and getting light. I was shivering, partly from the cold and partly, no doubt from fear, or at least apprehension. I knocked tentatively on the door. A moment or two passed and the door opened, slowly, to reveal a man in his mid-fifties wearing a beret and a bushy moustache. He was every inch the archetypal Frenchman; indeed he could not have looked more French if he had been wearing a string of onions around his neck.

I spoke briefly to him in French and explained I was 'un aviateur Anglais' who was very much in need of help. The farmer did not allow me into his home but told me to go back to the forest and hide and that he would find me later in the day. I did as I was told, returning to the forest to find temporary sanctuary and finishing off what remained of my escape rations. The farmer was good to his word. As dusk was falling, I could see him approach from my vantage point with a pair of bicycles. He gave me one of them and told me to follow him into a nearby village about a mile or so away. I pedalled anxiously behind him, feeling somewhat exposed in my RAF uniform and flying boots that instantly marked me out as an airman on the run.

We arrived in the village and stopped in a tiny square. My would-be helper pointed to a side street and said I was to go down and knock on the door of a particular house where more friends would be there to help me. I was by now very tired and my senses were dulled. It did not occur to me that it could be a trap. Perhaps it was all too easy; on reflection, possibly it was, and possibly I should have been more cautious. I cycled the few short yards to the house he had indicated, dismounted, and tentatively knocked on the door. A moment or two passed before I heard the bolt lift and the door opened.

I stared straight into the face of a man in SS uniform.

CHAPTER THREE

IN ENEMY HANDS

Gathering my senses, I spoke quickly to the man in German. He was, in fact, Dutch, and working for the local road authority. My fears of being betrayed, it seemed, had been unfounded and he said that he would help. He gave me bread to eat and something warm to drink, both of which were more than welcome; the past few hours had been exhausting and I felt incredibly tired.

I was still somewhat nervous about my new friend, and though I could speak his language, I did not let on that I was fluent. I spoke slowly and deliberately 'badly'; I did not want him asking too many questions as regards how I had learned to speak German so well. It might not be to my advantage to say I had been born in Berlin. We had what would now be described as a 'healthy debate'. I told him that the war was lost, that an invasion was just around the corner and the Germans might as well pack up and go home. I had a packet of English cigarettes on me and we shared them between us. It was all rather surreal and, I realised later, very much the lull before the storm.

While I smoked I thought. I thought about the rest of my crew, and whether anyone else had made it out alive. I had seen Bob bale out, of course, and wondered if he, like me, had been captured, or whether he was at the very moment on the run, and planning his escape back to England. Barry I knew had been killed, I had been standing right next to him when it happened, but what of the others? I had seen our aircraft crash and explode, and anyone who was still onboard at the time could not have survived the impact. It was a depressing thought. For the moment, however, I had to think of myself. My new Dutch friend had to work, and promised he would return with friends when he came off duty in the morning.

Three others in the crew had in fact made it out of the stricken bomber – the wireless operator, flight engineer and navigator. Brian Richards was always under the impression that their aircraft had been hit by flak in the bomb bay. The flight engineer, Jack Camp, similarly stated that they had been 'hit by a rocket' on the port side at the rear. He baled out and landed in a ploughed field south-east of Amiens.

When Bob Wallace baled out, he discovered that only one part of his parachute harness was properly attached but he still landed safely. The fact that other members of the crew believed they had been the victim of flak rather than a fighter is not unusual, especially since they had been shot down by an upward-firing cannon which went by the name of 'Schräge Musik' (literally 'slanting music' or 'Jazz'). Nightfighter pilots using 'Schräge Musik' would attack from below the bombers, hence why they were so rarely seen. The Halifax crashed on the territory of the commune of La Ferté-Saint-Samson. The three crewmen who were killed were all buried at the Poix-de-la-Somme churchyard, Somme, France.

Left on my own, I worried about Jean and home, and all that I had left behind. I knew that our loss would have now been reported, and telegrams despatched to our next of kin to say that we were missing and that further news would follow. Wing Commander Forsyth would be signing letters, written almost certainly by his adjutant, to tell our loved ones what splendid chaps we all were, and that although our time on the squadron had only been short, we had made an excellent impression with our keenness for getting to grips with the enemy. It was all nonsense of course. I doubt if he remembered half of us[16].

At Leconfield, the ever-efficient 'standing committee of adjustment' would have moved in, stripped our beds, and removed our kit and personal effects so that the next crew could move in. I remembered this process well; we shared a block with a crew that went missing, and the speed with which their lives were all but erased from the squadron was alarming, and we resented the 'new boys' who now occupied their beds, much as the more experienced crews had resented us on our arrival. I wondered whether my personal items would be auctioned off, as was customary in our squadron. Individuals paid over the odds for the smallest of items, raising as much money as we could for the families of the deceased. I had loaned Barry some money, against which he had given me his camera as collateral. I knew I would never see either the money or the camera again.

The storm came in the early morning with a screech of brakes and the arrival of a Kübelwagen with three men in it, as well as a young man in the distinctive uniform of the Hitler Youth – the organisation that I had been banned from joining a lifetime before. The atmosphere very quickly changed. Whereas the Dutch SS man had been calm and comparatively considerate – given I was the enemy – these new men were completely the

---

16   The letter sent to at least two other members of the crew was identical, save for the change in names. Forsyth did indeed write that the crew '.... were an inspiration to us all'.

opposite, and I realised very quickly that I was now in the hands of the Gestapo (the German secret police). I was pleased that my dog tags did not reveal my true religion.

The fact that I had been betrayed took a little while to dawn on me. There was nowhere to run; no escape possible. In a way I was relieved. I did not blame the Dutchman for handing me over. I did not think of him as a traitor or collaborator. Holland and France were occupied territories, and many just wanted to get on with their lives without interference from friend or foe. And I was a hindrance. I did not doubt for one moment that if England had been occupied, many British people would have behaved similarly.

They immediately started to shout and bellow instructions, both at me and the Dutchman, and their mood was not improved when I told them that I wasn't deaf and there was no need to shout. This only served to excite them further, and discretion being the better part of valour I decided to keep quiet and see what transpired.

I was bundled into the car and driven to Rouen, which was the nearest big town to where I had been picked up. The area was teeming with German troops wearing all manner of military uniforms, and I learned that it was a major rest and recreation area for officers and men seeking solace from their provincial villages and air bases. I was taken to German military headquarters and unceremoniously thrown into a cell. I was kept in the cell for only a short time before being transferred to the local police headquarters where I had a happy reunion with my wireless operator, Brian Richards. Brian, like me, looked somewhat dishevelled and the worse for wear but otherwise was in one piece. I think we both shared in that brief moment of relief at seeing a friendly face.

We were not in the police headquarters long before once again being moved, this time to the Luftwaffe HQ in the town. We were locked in separate cells for the night. Over the next 24 hours my solitude was frequently interrupted by a period of interrogation and verbal assaults. At no stage during this interrogation was I physically harmed, but the threat of violence was always hanging in the air.

Having decided I was of little use to them, I was taken from my prison cell with Brian and an escort of four guards to the local railway station where we caught a train to Paris. At Paris we disembarked, and marched to another platform and another train. By this time, some of my confidence had returned, and somewhat buoyed by being among French people I began to shout "Vive La France" at the top of my voice. At that point I received a clip around the head from one of the guards and was told to keep quiet.

We boarded another train – still in the company of the same four guards – for a destination that was as yet still unknown to me. On the train I was given my own compartment with half of my escort, away from the rest of the passengers. The train was especially crowded, however, and I was certainly not the most popular man on board. We were by now in the fifth year of the bombing war and the frequency and might of the bombing campaign was virtually at its height. Thousands of civilians were being killed or made homeless every week, and it was no wonder that there was no love for people – such as me – who had brought them such misery.

A German officer (a major) came into our compartment to remonstrate with my guards. How was it, he demanded to know, that a *'terrorflieger'*[17] was allowed to sit in comparative luxury, when all around him the people he terrorised were obliged to stand, and a major had nowhere to sit? He was not a happy man, but soon after calmed down when I began speaking to him in German and agreeing with his point of view. This seemed to diffuse the situation entirely and with the guard's permission he was invited in to share our space. We talked then for most of the journey, and he shared his rations – bread and sausage – with us as we discussed the progress of the war.

The train pulled into Frankfurt station and we were again escorted under close protection onto a tram that would take us to our final destination, Oberursel. I was pleased to have the German guards with me, for the looks I received from the citizens of Frankfurt were far from friendly. Indeed they were positively hostile, and I had no doubt whatsoever that given half a chance they would happily butcher me where I stood. I kept my head down and (unusually) my mouth shut.

Oberursel was the location of a *Durchgangslager Luft* (Dulag Luft) – a Luftwaffe interrogation centre through which all allied airmen prisoners of war would pass before being sent to a prisoner of war camp. The Dulag Luft had been set up to squeeze every last ounce of information from aircrew who were often still in a state of shock, and ready to talk.

I was once again placed in solitary confinement, having first been stripped, searched, and my particulars taken down and noted. My new home had little by way of any comforts. Indeed it had none. There was a bed but no lavatory – not even a bucket. When you needed to go, there was a slat by the door that you could open as a signal that you needed some attention.

---

17 Literally 'terror flyer' – a term repeatedly used by the German propaganda minister Joseph Goebbels.

It was then at the gift of your gaolers as to whether you were let out or left to suffer the ignominy of soiling yourself.

I was to learn very quickly that this was all part of the 'interrogation' in its broadest sense. Later I would hear stories of men locked in rooms where the heating was turned up to such levels as to be unbearable. Then the heating was switched off altogether and the men froze. Such tactics were all designed to weaken your resistance and loosen your tongue.

In my case, the methods deployed were rather more predictable. I would at first be questioned by a man who shouted and threatened me with violence. He would say that I was alone, and that no one knew of my existence or whether I was safe. On that basis, he could make me disappear; I could be shot and no one would be any the wiser. No sooner had he finished than another man would start and apologise for his colleague's behaviour. He would say that the rest of them disliked him too, and that he had every sympathy with my predicament. Then he would attempt through kindness to tease out of me what information he could.

Everyone took to interrogation differently. Some men offered nothing more than name, rank and number, like we had been taught. Some did not even offer that. Others were prepared to talk at length, to discuss tactics and aircraft, as though they were talking to fellow airmen with a shared interest. I was somewhere in-between. At first, I spoke only to confirm the basics. But as the interrogation went on, I could see no harm in answering questions such as who was my favourite composer or author. What I did not know, necessarily, was how skilled these interrogators were. Everything you said beyond name, rank and number allowed them to build up a picture of your character and make-up, and with that they might find chinks in your armour.

What I was not prepared for, however, was the level of detailed information they already had about me and my squadron. They knew my aircraft, my commanding officer, my flight commander, and various characters both on and off the base associated with our flying careers. Of course they watched to see how you responded; a look of surprise at the mention of a particular name or incident might be enough to confirm a suspicion that they already had. I began to see why saying nothing at all was probably the safest bet.

At various points they tried to reach me in other ways. On one of my first nights in solitary, I could hear tapping on the pipes in the neighbouring cell. I realised that it was Morse code, and that the cell's occupant was attempting to make contact with me. I was immediately on my guard, and save for a few basic pleasantries, decided to keep quiet. One afternoon I was interviewed by an RAF squadron leader who spoke with an Irish accent. I have no idea to this day whether this man was a fake, or bona fide, but anyhow he issued me with a form and asked me to fill it out. The form purported to be from the International Red Cross (IRC), and I was told that unless and until I answered the questions, my next of kin would not know of my whereabouts and they would not be able to communicate with me once I reached a permanent camp. The first few questions seemed fair enough, but as I read through the document, it became clear that the information they were looking for about my aircraft, my target, the bomb load, fellow crew members etc could not have come from the IRC. Only an idiot would have filled out the form and I was certainly not an idiot. The Irish officer was not best pleased.

I had been at Dulag Luft in captivity for less than a week[18] when I was approached by the main German interpreter and asked if I would like to go for a ride. I was both intrigued and suspicious in equal measure and so consulted the senior British officer (SBO), Flight Lieutenant Herbert Moore[19]. Moore was happy for me to go, and so later that day I found myself being driven to a small hunting lodge on the outskirts of Frankfurt. It was clear very quickly that it was a radio station, and it was equally clear that they expected me to broadcast home. It immediately crossed my mind how amusing it might be for me, a Jew, to be broadcasting across the German airwaves, but I politely declined and was soon after driven back to the camp.

On my return, the SBO sent for me. He had learned that I spoke Russian, and one of the officers' camps was in need of a Russian interpreter. For some reason I thought that an officers' camp may have been more comfortable than a camp for NCOs, and so said I would give it my consideration. The sticking point was that as an NCO, I would be obliged to stay in an officers' camp as an orderly, and did not much fancy spending my time serving others or cleaning the latrines. I said that I would go, but only if the SBO wrote a letter that said I was there as an interpreter, and was to be excused orderly's duties. He agreed. Soon after, I found myself on the way to my first permanent prison home: Stalag Luft III in Zagan (Sagan), Poland.

With the exception of Colditz, Stalag Luft III is probably today the most famous of all prisoner-of-war camps, but at the time it was just an assortment

---

18 According to official records, Andy was imprisoned at Dulag Luft between April 26 – April 29.
19 Moore had been a pilot with 619 Squadron, shot down on operations to Aachen on the night of April 11/12, 1944. His Lancaster was hit and burst into flames. Only Moore and his wireless operator managed to make it out in one piece, to survive as prisoners of war.

of ordinary-looking wooden huts, all uniform in appearance, behind a barbed wire fence, surrounded by pine trees and home to thousands of allied airmen of all nationalities. Unlike many of my contemporaries, I arrived at Zagan in a lorry from the station. More often than not, prisoners were obliged to walk, having been confined in cattle trucks for hours and sometimes days at a time. Taken through the gates, I was duly processed by the camp authorities. This comprised a series of checks and investigations about my person including – again – being asked to strip (something I was now getting used to). My fingerprints and photographs were taken, and I was given an official 'number' – in my case 4064. Only after all of this was completed, was I escorted into the camp properly.

When Zagan had first opened in 1942, it had been intended to house all shot down and captured airmen. It was also considered escape proof. Two spectacular escapes had quickly put paid to that myth. The first was the famous 'Wooden Horse' incident, where three POWs had hidden inside a vaulting horse that was carried out into the compound every day for gymnastics. While their colleagues exercised, the three men beneath the horse dug a tunnel. In time, the tunnel was of sufficient length that they were able to make a break, and all three men successfully made it back to England.

The second, and even more famous attempt, was the so-called 'Great Escape' in which 76 prisoners of war escaped from a tunnel on the night of March 24/25, 1944. Of their number, three men made a successful 'home run' but 50 others were recaptured and shot on the direct orders of Adolf Hitler. I arrived in Zagan just a few weeks after the escape and just a few days after news of the murders had been announced. Indeed the fate of some of those who had escaped that night was still not known. (While some had been returned to Zagan, a number were still effectively 'missing'. They would later be accounted for in a variety of different scenarios, including a handful of the most persistent escapers who were at that time rotting in Sachsenhausen concentration camp.)

It is difficult to describe the state of shock that was evident in the camp at that time. Until then, escape – to many at least – had been something of a game, an activity to exercise both the mind and the body, a duty to outwit the enemy, to win and not be beaten, to somehow continue the fight. After the Great Escape, and the murder of 'the fifty' in cold blood, the mood changed. Some became more determined than ever that they must do everything in their power to upset the German war machine; others resigned themselves to the fact that the rules had changed and that escape was no longer practical or desirable. Into the middle of this depressing scene entered one Sergeant

Weizman, a Polish national, a Jew, flying in a Royal Australian Air Force squadron, to all intents and purposes a foreigner who was not to be trusted.

Every new prisoner entering the camp was immediately interrogated by the camp's own RAF intelligence people. They wanted to know where I was from, where I had been shot down, what had happened to the rest of my crew and so on. I was reluctant to answer, which only added to their suspicions of someone with a strange accent and less than Anglo-Saxon appearance. They wanted detail on the progress of the war, and I was pleased to be able to tell them that the invasion was just around the corner and that the war would doubtless soon be over. Of course they had heard this all before; some of the men had been prisoners for more than four years and had lost count of the occasions they had prayed that the war would indeed be over by Christmas.

Such caution was understandable, if a little tiresome. Stool pigeons and traitors were rare but not unheard of. The Germans were not averse to attempting to turn or blackmail captured aircrew into helping them, and the prisoners needed to be on their guard. There was always a suspicion, albeit a very slight one, that the Germans had known all along about 'Tom', 'Dick' and 'Harry', the three tunnels built as part of the Great Escape 'campaign', and hadn't one of them been discovered when they were only weeks away from completing it?

This caution manifested itself in the form of my own escort, a squadron leader. Though I cannot now recall his name, he was with me 24 hours a day, and I was not allowed to speak or integrate with any of the other prisoners until I had been vetted. This meant we did everything together, and I mean everything. We ate, slept and shat as one; I was never out of his sight. The vetting procedure was simple: if there was a Kriegie in the camp who could vouch for you, that was good enough. But for the first few days there was nobody I recognised or who recognised me, and this was not helped by the fact that I was an NCO in the officers' compound (the NCOs and the officers were kept separate, albeit they were in the same overall establishment). At last among a new batch of airmen who marched into the camp one morning, was a chap with whom I had trained in South Africa. I was finally allowed to cast off my shadow.

Many books have been written by prisoners of war recounting their experiences of camp life. Most agree that the biggest enemy was boredom. One quickly settled into the routine of prison life: the routine of 'appels', the roll calls that required us to stand out in all weathers, on parade, sometimes for several hours until the Germans had completed their count; the routine of mealtimes, learning to divide our meagre rations of black bread, rotting potatoes and watery soup that was meant to sustain us, but did little or nothing to assuage our hunger; and the routine of our ablutions, comprising only one lukewarm shower every few weeks and the rest of the time we were expected to wash in the coldest of cold water.

My father had taught me a valuable lesson as a youngster: he said that if you ever find yourself in a tough situation, you had to think about your predicament, analyse it, and work out if there was a way of making that situation better. If, after your analysis, you were powerless to improve your lot, then you simply had to accept it, not worry about it, and move on. I took this exact approach in the camp, but in many ways I was lucky. Because I was used to my own company, and was not especially bothered by sport or games, the fact that we were often denied such activities was not a hardship. Others felt differently; they felt restrained. They needed to exert themselves physically or else they would go mad.

Living with so many strangers in such close proximity was certainly difficult, and you learned to be tolerant. Some wanted to sleep; others to play bridge; another to play his saxophone which had arrived, courtesy of the YMCA which, along with the Red Cross and their magnificent food parcels, was our lifeline to the outside world. Indeed without these food parcels, many prisoners would have starved, for as the war progressed, and the situation in the east became more desperate for the Germans, what little food they gave us seemed to get less and less by the week.

Our typical day started with a reveille of sorts, the Germans banging loudly on the doors and opening the shutters on the windows to let in the pale and insipid light of dawn. As one of the new boys, I had been allocated the bottom bed on a two-tier bunk. Above me was a large Dutchman, who each morning would swing his legs over the edge of the mattress and use whatever part of me that was protruding to propel himself onto the floor. He would then put on his homemade wooden clogs (shoes and boots were in short supply) and stump across the room to the window, and throw it open. He would then spit out a huge globule of phlegm and mutter "another f**king day in this f**king country", then return to his bed and use my body once again to clamber back into the top bunk and endeavour to sleep some more. After three days of this, I decided I would have a word. I told him it was getting on my nerves. "Look Andy," he said, "you talk too much and that's getting on my nerves, so let's learn to live together." It didn't seem to bother me after that.

This ritual completed, it was time for one of our number to fetch breakfast that comprised a loaf of thick black German bread. This is not bread in the sense that people would understand today, but rather a black brick whose principal ingredient appeared to be sawdust. Nevertheless, how the bread was divided became an art and in some groups it became an obsession. Our routine was to take it in turns to be the 'slicer', and the one who sliced chose last. That way we all did our utmost to ensure each portion was equal and fair. On the bread we might spread a little *'ersatz'* (imitation) margarine or jam, if it were available, all washed down with a mug of revolting coffee. (Hot water, however, was always in short supply so the option was sometimes whether to drink it or use it to shave).

After breakfast appel, many would return to bed to read, or take a walk around the compound where they talked and dreamed of home. Some would work in the theatre; some would tend meagre gardens growing radishes and cucumbers from seeds sent to them by the YMCA or Red Cross; others would sunbathe (when the weather allowed); some went to lectures (we had all manner of experts within the camp from architects to zoologists) or write up their diaries in notebooks that had been given to us specifically for the purpose. The important thing was to keep your mind active, and not allow yourself time to dwell.

We eked out the morning until lunchtime, our repast depending mainly on the state of the Red Cross parcels. Most rooms had a communal cook and would share their provisions. Others were more selfish and did not, jealously guarding what little they had for themselves. Whatever we did we did slowly; there was never any rush. As Winston Churchill wrote of his experiences as a prisoner of war in 1899: 'the days are long; the hours crawl by like paralytic centipedes'.

A typical afternoon might be spent debating the progress of the war in front of a huge, hand-drawn map with our best guess as to the Allies' advances. We all became perfect strategists who could have won the war at a stroke had we been left in charge. In the evening we would return to our huts for an evening meal. Soon after, with loud shouting and more banging the shutters would be closed and we would be locked in for the night, for the same routine to begin again the following morning.

Occasionally we were allowed a hot shower, and an incident there led to my first spell in solitary confinement. Left waiting in a queue for some time, and with little sign of progress, I started to sing a version of the German national anthem. Rather than suggest, however, that Germany was 'uber alles in der Welt', I sang 'uber Germany the RAF'. Unsurprisingly they were not best pleased with my lack of respect. I was unceremoniously hauled out of the line and marched off for seven days on my own, in a cell (the infamous 'cooler'), to contemplate my misdemeanour. Unfortunately, the others were also denied a shower, and I was not universally popular.

For me, solitary was not a hardship: you were excused appels and had ample time to read and enjoy your own company. Others found it a terrific ordeal, especially those who had been in the camp for some time (some of my contemporaries had been 'in the bag' since 1939), or who were 'wire happy'. We all coped with our captivity in different ways. I recall one RAF officer who appeared mad, and insisted that he be carried to appel in a wooden box. He would dutifully sit in this box until counted, and then insist that he be carried back to his hut. The whole process of counting prisoners was also slightly insane; we assembled as huts, in lines of three, and it was not difficult to disrupt the count if we needed. Indeed there was quite a bit of sport to be had when required.

We ate, slept and paraded together as huts, and each hut thought they were superior to the next. We certainly did. Each hut also had its own senior officer, and ours was Lieutenant Commander Casson[20]. John Casson was regular Royal Navy, and therefore disliked me on two counts: firstly because I was in the junior service; and secondly because I was only in for the duration. We were obliged to follow his lead because of his rank, but that did not mean we had to like him. We clashed on more than one occasion.

The camp had characters of all nationalities: Australians; Poles; Czechs, some using assumed names. (I myself had 'anglicised' my name from Weizman to Wiseman – an action that seemed prudent at the time.) The Poles amused me by dressing for bed, sometimes complete with hairnets. Most were regulars, and fastidious in their appearance. One hut captured a mouse and had it court-martialled for eating food supplies. The mouse was found guilty and sentenced to 14-days solitary on bread and water. After its release, it was adopted as a pet and fed three times a day in a cage built for the purpose.

Along with our food parcels, our other lifeline was of course the mail. Through the auspices of the Red Cross, my fiancée Jean was now able to write to me at Zagan. She had my address, the official prison camp designation, and my own individual number. I also received news about my mother. My

---

20 Casson had been the commanding officer of 803 Naval Air Squadron, flying Blackburn Skuas from the deck of the *Ark Royal*. He had been one of eight aircraft shot down while attacking German capital ships in Trondheim harbour in June 1940, during the Norwegian campaign. Casson, and his observer Peter 'Hornblower' Fanshawe, had played a key part in the Great Escape, Fanshawe being credited with inventing the 'trouser bags' to disperse sand from the three tunnels under construction.

mother was in Poland, and would write to a friend of hers in Switzerland who would in turn pass on the news to me via Jean. In many ways, I did not want to hear from my mother.

I appreciate writing these words today that this might sound insensitive or even callous, but it was a part of my life that I had completely shut down. I had not heard from my father since the day that I arrived in the UK and did not learn of his fate until I was reunited with my mother in July 1945. He perished in the camps, one of the countless millions of victims of the Holocaust. My mother survived initially because she was a US citizen. In marrying my father, however, she surrendered her nationality. (Before the US entered the war, she applied to have her passport returned to her from the US Embassy in Berlin. They would not send it to her, however. She was obliged to go the embassy in person to collect it, but the German authorities in Poland would not allow her the necessary permits to travel.) Fortunately, while at university in St Petersburg she had obtained a certificate to say that she was a Lutheran, and this was infinitely better than being a Polish Jewess.

I can admit that I was not an especially popular prisoner, at least not with my fellow NCOs. I did not do the duties of an orderly, which I believe annoyed them, and I could no doubt come across as awkward at times. I was always told that the most important English word was 'why' but found that forever asking 'why' was not something that endeared you to others, particularly not others in the service. My purpose in being in the officers' compound was to act as interpreter, and to this end I was one of a team of about half a dozen who spoke fluent German, but I was the only one who spoke Russian. This was to prove vital in the months that followed.

The duties of an interpreter were many and varied. First and foremost we would accompany the senior British officer at every meeting with our German hosts to ensure that everything that was said was properly communicated and understood – by all sides. These meetings could be difficult; Oberst Von Lindeiner, the camp commandant at the time of the Great Escape, had been removed in disgrace. A gentleman of the old school who wore the 'Pour le Mérite' decoration at his throat, he had been held directly accountable for failing to prevent the breakout and fell foul of the rivalry between Goering, the head of the Luftwaffe, and Himmler, the head of the SS and Gestapo, for control over allied prisoners of war. Lindeiner was well thought of by the senior RAF officers within the camp, but his replacement, Oberst Franz Braune, an elderly, craggy-faced man, was more of an unknown quantity. What we did know was that he did not speak any English at all, and so our services were in constant demand. Braune was something of a contradictory personality. He appeared totally devoid of any humour or emotion and yet was reportedly appalled at the shooting of 'the fifty', allowing the surviving Kriegies to construct a memorial to their honour, a memorial to which he also lent his personal support. It was Braune who had the sad duty of informing the SBO of the murders.

In the same way that there had been change at the top in command of the Germans, so too had there been change amongst the senior British officers. Group Captain Hubert Massey, a much admired and respected leader, had been repatriated. (Indeed I believe it was Massey who was responsible for bringing the murders of 'the fifty' to the attention of the British government.) An Australian, Group Captain Douglas Wilson RAAF, took over as the senior officer. Wilson had been the station commander at Holme-on-Spalding-Moor who decided to join a 76 Squadron crew for a trip to Mülheim in June 1943 and was shot down for his troubles.

Wilson had been an army lieutenant and was in the first group of a dozen or so men to go though the RAAF's new flying course (1FTS) in 1923. His service number, 16, reflected his seniority. Having graduated from RAF Staff College he commanded various squadrons before being promoted to command RAAF Station Richmond between 1939-40. He was later appointed senior administrative staff officer at RAAF Central Area Headquarters in Sydney, and was sent on exchange to the RAF in 1943 as OC RAF Wyton, RAF Linton-on-Ouse and, ultimately, Holme-on-Spalding-Moor. He died in August 1950.

As well as attending all meetings, as translators we were also given German newspapers to read and translate, issuing summaries of the key news to be distributed throughout the camp. On occasions I was permitted to listen to German radio broadcasts and again summarise the main events. This was then compared to the BBC news and an assessment made of the true picture. We were not permitted radios, of course, but over time parts were either stolen or smuggled into the camp and basic radio sets were constructed and concealed in secret hides. A team of news gatherers would create a daily bulletin that was then read out to each hut – without the Germans' knowledge – and then destroyed. In this way the prisoners were able to keep up with the progress of the war.

The methods we used as translators and the techniques deployed could vary. There was a pool of us, as I have said, and we were usually told where and when our skills were required, and when a meeting had been requested.

In advance of any formal meeting, the SBO would outline to us what he was looking to achieve, so that we had a broad picture of the words and the tone that we should adopt. Translating is not simply just about the words you use, but as much about how you use them, and the 'mood' you are looking to convey. Over time, the individual we were translating for would find a rhythm, speaking in short sentences or breaking longer sentences down into smaller parts, much as you would if you were asking someone to repeat what you were saying. In some meetings, individual words were often lost in the passion of how they were expressed. It is obvious in any language whether a man is angry or upset; the skill was in combining that passion with a clear message that led to the outcome you were looking for.

As well as acting in a 'formal' capacity, we each of us would help in 'local' disputes or conversations on a more day-to-day basis. In these cases, we rarely translated word for word, but rather used our own words to put across the grievance we had. It could be a grumble about a Red Cross parcel being interfered with, or the quality of the potatoes. For a period after the Great Escape, the prisoners' letters were stopped, and this was a constant source of frustration.

The most difficult task was the one allotted to me by the X organisation. This was in effect the escape committee, a group of die-hard officers determined to cause their German hosts maximum trouble. Roger Bushell, the larger-than-life fighter pilot and inveterate escaper had been the original 'Big X'. He had been murdered, one of 'the fifty'. His second in command, Wing Commander John Ellis, had since taken over, and set about rebuilding both the confidence and the capabilities of his escaping colleagues.

John Ellis had joined the RAF in March 1936 and on the outbreak of war had been posted to 610 Squadron, seeing considerable action over Dunkirk and winning his first DFC. He had been awarded a second by the end of the Battle of Britain, by which time he had shot down 11 enemy aircraft and taken command of the squadron. Posted to the Desert Air Force, he saw action in command of the Krendi Wing, flying from Malta. He suffered engine failure during operations to support the invasion of Sicily in June 1943, and was posted missing, later turning up at Stalag Luft III.

You could divide the camp almost exactly in half between those who wanted to escape, and those who wanted to see out the war in peace and quiet. I was somewhere down the middle. I knew that I could never be a tunnel man, but the idea of escape still held an appeal. In the event my mind was made up for me. One day, not long after I had been 'accepted' into the camp, I was sent for by the SBO. With some trepidation I knocked on the door of his room, entered and was told to sit down. Rather genially he asked me how I was settling down. I told him so far so good. He said that I had been 'observed', and that perhaps I should calm down a little. He was concerned that as a Jew, I would do better by blending into the background, and not drawing attention to myself. Then almost in the same breath he seemed to talk his own argument around, suggesting that because I was so outwardly-eccentric, nobody could possibly take my behaviour as anything other than an act. He then told me that he had bad news. Given my now better knowledge of British and indeed air force culture, I merely enquired, "Sir?" He replied: "I know you will take it on the chin, but because of your knowledge of foreign languages and your importance to us, I am going to have to order you not to try and escape. I am sorry, but that's how it is." Secretly I was not disappointed.

In the immediate aftermath of the Great Escape, and the murders, there had been much debate over whether these attempts to escape should continue. Posters had gone up declaring that escaping was no longer a sport and that prisoners if caught would be shot. No such threats seemed to intimidate the British for long, however, although by the time I arrived escaping was not yet fully back on the agenda. As one officer once said: "we were not so much prisoners of war, but rather prisoners *at* war."

A crucial part of any escape plan was information: information about railways stations; train times; movement orders; documents and travel permits. Getting out of the camp was only one part of the equation; putting as much distance between the escaper and his German captors in as short a time as possible was key, and this required careful planning.

This was part of what was formally known as the 'contact' system and one of my roles was essentially blackmail, plain and simple. Each of the interpreters would be allocated an individual guard whom we would befriend. We would talk about their families, their children, what they did before the war and what they hoped to do once the war was over and generally build up a rapport while all the time assessing whether they could be susceptible to a bribe. My contact was my own responsibility, and while he was being 'worked', no-one else was allowed to approach him. In the 1960s film, *The Great Escape,* one of the key roles with which I could identify was 'the scrounger' played by James Garner, for this was exactly how it was.

Perhaps, unintentionally, I made rather a good blackmailer and scrounger. I say 'unintentionally' because for me it wasn't really an act. I was genuinely interested in talking to the guards and actually grew to like one or two of them. These men were not crack troops of course, but usually elderly reservists or youngsters with ailments or disabilities that kept them from the frontline. And there were a good many of them: at one time the camp housed in excess of 10,000 prisoners of war of all nationalities (British, American, French, Dutch, Norwegian, Polish, Czechs etc. as well as the Commonwealth countries) with more than 2,000 Germans to guard us, and these guards were often rotated. Their biggest fear was a posting to the Russian front, and they would do everything to prevent that from happening. Sometimes I felt rather bad about using information against them to get what we wanted, as it was not in my nature to be 'nasty'.

My 'boss' during this time was Squadron Leader Waterer[21], the officer in charge of contacts. My official role was not only to secure information that could be of benefit to a potential escape, but also to glean any military intelligence that I could in terms of secret weapons, defences and morale. I was also tasked with securing all manner of articles from files and chisels through to petrol and wire, as well as various special metals acquired, to order. I did not ask questions. Neither did I ask any questions when acting as a 'watcher' for Wing Commander Ellis and his men. Hardly a day went by when there wasn't some form of subversive activity underway to keep us all on our toes.

By the autumn of 1944, it was clear to everyone that the war was going badly for the Germans. That was reflected partly in their attitude toward us, which went steadily downhill. Guards who were by nature happy became morose. Those who were already morose became petty, and inclined to bully. My contact role that until that point had meant engaging the Germans was expanded to include contact with the Soviets, helping to keep our senior officers better informed.

On one morning in October, I was on duty to escort Group Captain Wilson who had requested a meeting with Oberst Braune. Wilson explained to Braune in clear and precise tones that it was evident that the war was coming to an end and that the Red Army was getting closer by the day. With that point made and understood, he stated that the prisoners wished to stay in the camp and wait to be liberated by their advancing armies.

Braune listened respectfully while I translated and then gave his reply. He could not, he explained, accede to our request unless ordered to do so by Berlin. If Berlin said we were to stay, we would stay. If Berlin ordered

---

21   An experienced navigator, Squadron Leader Gomer Waterer had been the navigation leader at 35 Squadron, Pathfinder Force. He had been shot down while attacking Nuremberg on the night of March 8/9, 1943, flying with Flying Officer John Brown. Their victor was Oberleutnant Ludwig Meister of 1/ NJG4 who survived the war with 35 victories.

that we would move, we would move. We understood his position and the interview came to an end. Braune's hands were tied and our fate was sealed.

We spent a miserable Christmas at Zagan. There did not seem much to celebrate. It was freezing cold and there was snow falling all around. Had we a thermometer to tell us the temperature, it would have read minus 20. Everything was frozen including, for a time at least, our spirit. Because of the effectiveness of our bombing war, much of the German rail and transport infrastructure had been damaged or destroyed, and this severely hampered the flow of any mail into the camp. Of far greater concern, however, was the absence of any Red Cross food parcels, for our food stocks were now in a parlous state.

The SBO had issued instructions through the network of compound leaders and hut leaders that we would soon be obliged to leave. He did not know when, and we did not know where we would be evacuated to, but that it was only a matter of time. These instructions led to a frenzy of activity among certain prisoners. Some saw the move as an opportunity for escape, and started to prepare accordingly. What little chocolate, butter and raisins that were left were boiled up into some glutinous mess, cooled and then cut into slabs. They looked and no doubt tasted disgusting, but they were packed with calories and intended to sustain the individual in the ordeal that was to follow. The fitter amongst us tried to get fitter still, ready for a quick dash, and could be seen running circuits around the camp. To me it all seemed like wasted energy.

There was a strange air of expectancy in the camp: part excitement; part fear. We knew that the Soviets were close, primarily from the reports on the radio. But soon we did not need a third party and the dulcit tones of a BBC announcer to tell us the good news, for we could hear the Red Army guns for ourselves. One Saturday morning (January 27), I went with the group captain to the kommandant's office. Braune explained, and I translated, that he had received orders from Berlin that we were not to be moved. This was joyous news, for we did not wish to be moved. But our joy was short-lived. Later that evening we were summoned again and told that the order had been countermanded. The group captain was furious, and protested in the strongest terms that we should be allowed to stay. The kommandant would not, or could not, tell us where we were being moved to, and this served only to further heighten the group captain's concern for our future safety.

We had good reason to be concerned. In war there is always confusion, and at that precise moment the Germans were in a particularly confused state. I believe they could not tell us where we were being sent because at that time they simply did not have the answer other than 'away from the Russians'. There was, we later learned, a plan to move all allied prisoners of war to the areas surrounding Berlin and to the north and to be used as some sort of screen – what would be called today 'a human shield' – to disrupt the bombing offensive. There were other rumours, one that we did not dare contemplate, that orders had been given that all POWs would be shot.

It was by now after midnight, and we were given precisely two hours to pack up and be ready to go. This was an enormous task. Although we had always thought that this day would eventually arrive, it still came as a surprise. Prisoners who had been incarcerated for years had accumulated a large amount of personal kit that they were loathe to leave behind. They could only carry so much and so far, and for the time being we did not know how far we would have to travel.

The main priority was food and clothing, and to this end we were each given a Red Cross parcel that had been kept for this very reason. Indeed days before our departure, a consignment of parcels had arrived from Lübeck so we had gone from famine to feast virtually overnight. The difficulty now, of course, was that a Red Cross parcel was a sizeable object, and one that was not easy to carry. Some opted to get around this difficulty by fashioning home-made sleds of a simple yet effective design. The majority of us, however, went through our parcels, ate what we could there and then, and kept such food and clothing as we could realistically take with us. It meant throwing away such luxury items as marmalade and butter, for example, in preference for tins of spam and bars of chocolate.

We were determined, as far as possible, not to leave anything of value to the Germans, and set about destroying or spoiling what was left. Because of the amount of contraband involved this proved a near impossible task but that did not stop us from trying. One commodity that seemed to be in abundant supply was cigarettes and we soon learned the irony that you cannot set fire to a pile of cigarettes in one go. Instead we crushed them and stamped on them, and blocked the latrines with as many as we could before urinating on the remainder. It was on reflection a rather futile gesture but it certainly did not seem like that at the time. Cigarettes could be popular 'currency' and we did not want to make the Germans a present of them[22].

The compound was strewn with rubbish akin to the base camp at

---

22 Arthur Durand in his book *Stalag Luft III – A Secret History*, suggests that more than 25,000 Red Cross parcels had to be left behind.

Everest. Everywhere there were empty tins and cans, and discarded clothing. We formed up in huts, each hut assembling to form a much larger column until we were ready to march. I spoke to one of the guards and asked where we were heading but all that he could tell me was that it was westwards.

This was the start for us of what they now call 'The Long March' – a march that resulted in the deaths of a great many prisoners (and indeed their guards) who through a combination of exhaustion, malnutrition and hypothermia surrendered to the harsh conditions we had to face. It is misleading, I believe, to refer to it as a 'march', for at best we managed little more than a shuffle. Column upon column of ragged airmen, once in the prime of their lives but now looking like decrepit old men, wrapped up against the cold, their meagre belongings dragging behind. As we trudged, those who had miscalculated began discarding further items, leaving a trail of debris along the road, the flotsam and jetsam of prison life.

It was obvious immediately that there was little by way of any German plan or organisation behind our evacuation. No provisions in terms of food or water had been made for us and there was little or nothing by way of any shelter. That first day, with the snow still falling around us and the temperature below freezing (it was around minus 25) we passed through a number of hamlets and villages where the local people came out to stare at us and us at them with mutual suspicion. On occasion, we were given food, or able to barter in the time-honoured fashion exchanging one item for another. Elsewhere they would spit at us and hurl obscenities and stones for the misery and shame we had heaped upon their country.

The Geneva Convention, which gave us certain rights of protection, specified that prisoners were not to be made to march more than 20 kilometres a day, but the convention found few champions on those frozen roads and we marched until ordered to stop. On one brief respite I opened a tin of corned beef to find that it was harder than a block of ice and I could not bite into it.

We slept when we could, where we could: in churches; in schools; in the open. For one precious night I camped out in a glass factory where the furnaces were still burning. It allowed the medical officer to do what he could for the men in his charge, some of whom were suffering dreadfully with frostbite. On another night we slept on straw in a stable on the estate of the son of a famous Prussian general. The man in question was Generaloberst Hans Jurgen von Arnim who had succeeded Rommel as commander of the Afrika Korps in March 1943 and was captured two months later. This led to a rather extraordinary incident.

The Baroness von Arnim, the general's sister, heard that we were on her estate and sent word to invite our SBO for dinner. The old lady spoke English, but I was still invited along as interpreter, provided both Collard and I gave our parole[23]. The contrast of the rather magnificent baronial surroundings to what we had become accustomed to as prisoners was stark, and the food superb, served to us by French POWs who appeared to be on her staff. The conversation at dinner was polite and we took care not to mention the war and insult our host. She enquired whether our group captain had any mutual friends from days spent at Ascot or Wimbledon, but of course he did not and she seemed most disappointed. I assume she meant to appeal to him for protection for what must inevitably come.

While we were talking, one of the French household staff announced that a German officer had arrived and requested to speak to the baroness. He entered and said that he had come to take us back. The baroness reproached him. She said that we were her guests, and that *he* had not been invited. At that he did an about turn and skulked away.

The next morning and we were once again on the move, destination unknown. It was this uncertainty that began to get the better of some of us. It played on our minds, depressing our spirits and heightening our anxiety. Escape was now out of the question. There was simply no point. Our radio was still working, and the BBC broadcast an order that no further escape attempts were to be made. These orders were emphasised by the SBO. He had enough to put up with keeping the men and the walking wounded together, without having to contend with an irate German guard.

Rather fed up now with walking I asked the SBO whether he had further need of me for the day. When he said he did not, and I was confident that I wouldn't be missed, I started to fall to the rear of the column until they had passed. Notwithstanding our orders I then slipped away. It was an easy thing to do; the German guards were busy and I am not convinced they would have done much had they seen me. I could see a farmhouse close by, approached it and knocked on the door. The farmer and his wife were most hospitable. I told them I was lost and they invited me to sit by the fire, and fetched me some bread and a bowlful of soup. It was delicious. Sadly my brief moment of respite and familial comfort was not to last. The farmer had called the police – I had expected no less – and a Kübelwagen arrived to take me away. The police thanked me for not escaping and drove me back to the front of the column. I do not know what my fellow prisoners must have thought when they saw me, but I was none the worse for the experience. Indeed quite the opposite. I had some hot food inside me.

23 In effect an honourable promise not to escape for a limited period.

At last we reached the Saxon city of Spremberg and continued to the railway station. Signs of bomb damage were everywhere but the tracks still seemed to be complete and there was plenty of rolling stock of the type usually used to transport animals. That night was one of the more uncomfortable of the war. Not only were we out in the open, with no shelter, but we also found ourselves camped among soldiers of a tank training school – a rough-looking bunch, despite their youthful looks, who we had no intention of upsetting. We were, however, given water and soup, the first time I can remember being provisioned by our German guards since we left Zagan.

It was clear by now that Spremberg was not our final destination, and it was clear also that we were going to be divided. One party at least would be continuing north, towards the port of Bremen. The remainder was destined for Luckenwalde, a POW camp not far from Berlin. We had not rested long when the Germans started bellowing '*Raus Raus*' and we were herded – quite literally as it happens – onto the cattle trucks for our onward journey. There were more than 40 of us to each truck and the conditions were appalling. There was neither food nor water, and just a single bucket if anyone felt the urge or need to use it. But there was discipline. Despite the crowd, we were organised, taking it in turns to stand, crouch or lie down.

Our group finally arrived at Luckenwalde station at the end of the first week of February after a journey of several days. The doors were slid back, and we helped each other down onto the track. The Germans ordered us to assemble but of course we took little notice until instructed to do so by our own officers. A count was attempted but abandoned as the light continued to fade and the guards could not agree on a total. Without further ado we walked the short distance to the gates of Stalag Luft IIIA – the official designation for our new home – but were initially denied access. The guards said that the camp was full and that they could not take any more prisoners. We were not in the mood to listen and all but barged our way past them. Perhaps we should not have been so eager.

CHAPTER FOUR
A DANGEROUS TIME

Luckenwalde was little short of a disgrace. We had grown used to being deprived and did not expect the Ritz, but Luckenwalde was more squalid than we could have possibly imagined. The buildings were in a sorry state of repair with doors and windows hanging off their hinges and there was a smell of damp and decay. Inside, the huts were arguably worse; they were virtually uninhabitable and yet we were expected to bunk down 200 of us to a hut with little sanitation and no cooking facilities for what few provisions we had managed to save. Not surprisingly many men, already weakened by the forced march, fell victim to dysentery, and there were neither sufficient drugs nor food to improve matters.

Our contingent which had left Zagan now joined a much larger group of prisoners from many different nationalities: Russians; French; Italians; Americans; Poles. There was almost the entire Norwegian general staff, under the command of General Ruge, and we quickly learned their story. The Norwegians had all been sent home after their country had been invaded but some time later they were ordered to report to Oslo station with one suitcase each. They were subsequently transported to Germany as prisoners of war. Ruge was a gentleman of the old school. He was an elegant man, tall, grey hair, blue eyes, who had a delightful manner about him and spoke perfect English as only the Scandinavians can. In spite of his genial nature, I always thought I detected a slight sadness in him about having to surrender his country to the Germans. I may have been wrong, but it was an impression that I certainly had at the time.

The Norwegians in general were the most charming people and clearly had a like and respect for the British. They were the first to share with us some of their own Red Cross parcels. Not everyone was so enthusiastic or welcoming, however. The Americans appeared to lack any form of discipline and the Poles lived in perpetual fear of falling into Russian hands. The French – who had been in the camp the longest – were without question the worst. Their discipline was virtually non-existent. They did not lift a finger to help, despite having ample food parcels, most of which had been stolen. This seemed especially criminal given that some of our men were at starvation point. This may sound like exaggeration, but our daily ration (largely comprising barley soup, a thin slice of black bread and equally black potatoes) was estimated to be 600 calories below the minimum required to sustain life.

Keeping control of such a diverse mix of nationalities and cultures – a near impossible task – fell to General Ruge as the senior allied officer but he deferred to the senior British officer, who in the first instance was Group Captain Alfred Willetts DSO. Willetts had been the station commander at RAF Oakington who had insisted in accompanying a 7 Squadron crew for an attack on Berlin and been shot down for his troubles. He was in fact one of three station commanders lost that night. It was from Willetts that I first took my orders but he was not at Stalag Luft IIIA for long. Soon after he was replaced by one of the great, unsung heroes of the war, Wing Commander R C M Collard.

'Dickie' Collard was the man for the moment. He began organising the camp along pre-war RAF lines. The RAF effectively took over. There was an adjutant, a duty officer and daily orders posted on the noticeboard. Committees were formed and skilled workmen found among the Kriegies who could supervise and action repairs to the camp infrastructure – the huts, the electrics, the water etc. – and considerably improve conditions for all prisoners. The British had colonised a world, so a camp of our size was no problem.

Collard was a man everyone could respect. He wore the ribbons of the DSO and DFC and had the natural authority of a public-school-educated, regular RAF officer. He expected to be saluted and was. I liked him immediately, indeed we became friends, and he was quick to call upon my services for I was the only Russian speaker he could find amongst the RAF contingent. In short order, Collard had instilled discipline and order in the camp, but his rule of law was not universally accepted, particularly by the French who continued to cause us all difficulties.

Richard Charles Marler Collard – Dickie to his friends – was born on August 25, 1911, the son of a stockbroker. Educated at Haileybury, a school with a proud air force tradition, he joined the RAF in 1931, serving with 4 Squadron and 615 Squadron, becoming a flying instructor. On the outbreak of war he had been part of the Advanced Air Striking Force (AASF) in France and served a tour in the Middle East in command of 37 Squadron, seeing action in Greece, Albania, Italy, Iraq and Syria and was awarded the DFC. He added the DSO as OC 12 Squadron, his citation referring to his 'determination and exceptional devotion to duty' that had been 'an inspiration to everyone under his command'. He was shot down and taken prisoner on operations to Duisburg on July 25, 1942. After the war he led a goodwill tour of the United States and retired from the RAF as a group captain to enter politics. He died in 1962. Among his decorations, he received the Norwegian King Haakon VII's Cross of Liberty in recognition of his work in the camps.

On April 10, a rumour began circulating that we were going to be moved to a new camp near Munich. There was considerable consternation at the news and it was made very clear to the German authorities that any such move would not be with our co-operation. Despite the obvious futility, the Germans seemed determined, and 36 hours later a large contingent of Kriegies – myself and Dickie Collard included – was once again on the move, being marched down to the local railway station from whence we originally arrived. The departure was far from orderly, and a good many huts and their contents had been damaged in our haste to leave.

At the railway station we were ordered to board a series of goods wagons that had been arranged for our transport. Collard refused, unless and until some RAF roundels had been painted on the wagons to show that we were prisoners of war. Typhoon and Mosquito pilots were shooting up everything that moved on the railways and we had no intention of being killed by our own side so close to freedom. After much discussion and negotiation, in which I was closely involved, we finally got the Germans to agree. But the whole process had taken many hours, and by the time we were finally ready to depart, the line up ahead had been bombed so we were effectively blocked in. It was perhaps a good thing, for it was rumoured that we were bound for Bavaria. As it was, we were marched back to the camp, many regretting the damage they had wreaked for in many cases they now had nowhere to sleep and/or their bunks had been taken.

This was a dangerous time for all of us. We could tell by now that the Red Army was close; we could clearly hear their guns. Above us, the air war still raged and the Allies did not always have it all their own way. On more than one occasion we saw one of our own aircraft fall to the guns of a German fighter or flak and so the war was not yet won. Whereas our own guards may have been at the point of surrender, and many had already deserted, there were still pockets of fanatical SS troops and Hitler Youth nearby, and they would have shot us and the deserters out of hand given half a chance.

A fair few of us thought about escape. Conditions in the camp had improved (the Red Cross had somehow managed to get food through to us), but we were now in the front line. Our German hosts had become unpredictable, and there was the ever-present threat of retribution from the SS at the eleventh hour. Two RAF airmen tried to make a break for it on April 13 and were shot for their troubles[24].

The hours and days ticked slowly by and all we could do was wait. News reached us that the other half of our Zagan party had now been liberated and morale in our own camp soared. We had a grandstand seat for Bomber Command's last major raid of the war, an attack on Potsdam which created a spectacular firework display that belied the fact that perhaps as many as 5,000 German civilians were killed that night. Our numbers seemed to be swelling all the time and many were obliged to sleep in the open under whatever basic shelter we could provide. Then one morning it happened. The Germans left. One minute they were there, and the next they had gone – or at least that was how it seemed. It was April 21.

Almost at once, the well-oiled machinery of service discipline and organisation again manifested itself in a general order issued by General Ruge. This general order (number one) confirmed Ruge's authority and called upon all of us prisoners to demonstrate 'close collaboration and firm discipline so long as the present situation prevails'. He wrote: 'I therefore expect my efforts to safeguard the security of all personnel and the smooth running of the camp to be met with loyal support from all nations and all ranks.' The document outlined the 'liberty of movement', making it clear in principle that prisoners were not to leave their respective compounds. It set out how the compounds were to be policed, with the 'police' identified by white armbands with a green cross worn on their left sleeve. As an interpreter I was expected to wear a white armband with a green D on it whenever on duty.

Food was of course the greatest area of concern to all of us and was to be distributed on a communal basis. All food stores, including parcels, were to be issued on a pro rata basis to kitchens 'without regard to the source or consignee'. Food that was already in the hands of certain prisoners was not to be collected, but would be taken into account when any new food supplies were being allocated. In the event of an emergency, a single warning signal would be made, similar to that to warn of an air raid.

---

24 Wing Commander Roland Beamont in his diary suggests they were two NCOs and that one attacked a sentry with a bottle. The two are believed to be Flight Sergeant Percy Crosswell of 429 Squadron RCAF and Flight Sergeant Geoffrey Johnson of 158 Squadron RAF. Johnson died immediately; Crosswell lingered until 1030 hours on April 14 before finally succumbing to his wounds. Both were buried in the Luckenwalde camp cemetery but towards the end of the war, cemetery records were destroyed and many crosses removed or lost, leaving many graves unmarked and unregistered. Crosswell, posthumously commissioned pilot officer, is remembered on the Runnymede Memorial.

To complement the general order, Collard issued his own supplementary orders to all British personnel (I included myself in this case). Our personnel were divided into three 'units': officers and other ranks accommodated within the Oflag (*Offizier Lager*); RAF personnel accommodated within the Stalag; and army personnel within the Stalag. For each of these units, Collard appointed commanding officers: Wing Commander Eric Smith was in command of the Oflag; Wing Commander Roland Beamont DSO, DFC was in charge of the RAF men within the Stalag; and Squadron Leader 'Jock' Fielden, a former Royal Artillery officer, was given responsibility for the army. King's Regulations were to be imposed at all times.

Wing Commander Roland Beamont, a well-known fighter pilot, had been shot down by flak in October 1944 while commanding officer of the first Hawker Tempest Wing comprising 3, 486 and 56 Squadrons. He had fought in France in the winter of 1939/1940 with 87 Squadron, returning to the UK to take part in the Battle of Britain. 'Rested' as a test pilot for Hawkers, he flew the early Hawker Typhoon, helping to introduce the type into wartime service with 56 Squadron and then 609 Squadron, latterly as CO. After the war he became chief test pilot for English Electric, flying the prototype Canberra and Lightning, and establishing a cross Atlantic record in the Canberra.

Squadron Leader S S Fielden was shot down September 7, 1941 while flying with 12 Squadron on operations to Berlin. 'Jock' Fielden had flown Blenheims with 57 Squadron during the fall of France.

Wing Commander Eric Trenchard Smith was an Australian who had joined the RAF before the war and served in India, being decorated for service on the North West Frontier. He had been shot down in 1941.

The danger of our situation had still not passed. On the one hand, there was a certain euphoria at being 'free'. But on the other, we were still behind a barbed wire fence in a war zone, and not every German was intent on surrender. A wrong move now could prove fatal. One dawn I was lying in bed in a downstairs room of what had been the Kommandant's house when the field telephone rang. Dickie was fast asleep so I took it upon myself to answer the phone. Slowly and somewhat irritably I went over to the desk and picked up the receiver. It was an RAF officer at the main gate who sounded rather excited:

"There's a bloody great tank here," he said.
"It is Russian or German?" I replied
"I'm f***ed if I know, I'm flat on my face…"

To which I told him he had the wrong number and to phone back later.

Dickie by now was awake and asked what the phone call had been about. He said that I'd better get down to the main gate and find out what was going on. Wearily I pulled my boots on (we slept fully-clothed because of the cold) and Dickie said I could borrow his bicycle (it was a fair distance from the Kommandant's house to the gate). Just before I departed, he told me to write down Jean's telephone number in case anything happened to me. It wasn't the most reassuring send-off I could have wished for.

Pedalling towards the gate all manner of thoughts were going through my mind. If it were a Soviet tank, how would the Red Army soldiers behave and what would they demand of us? If it were a German, was there a danger that a mass killing was still on the cards? Some of our number had earlier raided the armoury and seized weapons and ammunition, and been obliged to turn them in. This was one powder keg that could yet explode in our faces.

Approaching the gate I could see that the vehicle was more of an armoured car than a tank, but I could still not make out whether it was friend or foe. I was never especially good at recognising different aircraft types so armoured vehicles were a mystery to me. Climbing off my bike I raised my arms and began shouting in Russian, German, French and English that we were British prisoners of war, and that the Germans had gone. There was nothing by way of reply, other than the rather disconcerting site of the gun turret following me as I moved. It sounds ridiculous now but my next move was to sit down on the ground in front of the vehicle, cross my legs, and reach out with both arms as if imploring them to help us. It was, I suppose, the ultimate symbol of submission that could and should be understood in any culture.

Slowly the hatch on top of the turret opened, and a figure in brown battledress emerged. It was a uniform I did not instantly recognise but knew that it was not German. The figure had a sub-machine gun around his neck, so I remained sitting until he spoke to me in Russian. The relief was indescribable, and very soon it was all smiles and laughter. I jumped onto the vehicle to greet him properly and we embraced. He was a Soviet lieutenant who had become temporarily detached from his unit and was now lost. He wanted to know where he was.

The RAF officer, who had by now recovered his composure, called Dickie to tell him all was well. The armoured vehicle then drove on, with me on board, to the Kommandant's house where Dickie had already organised a guard of honour to celebrate our salvation. The lieutenant produced a bottle of vodka and we in turn provided a map to show him where he was. With much back slapping and hugging (quite a challenge for some of the reserved British officers) he was soon after on his way again, this time to the cheers of many hundreds of Kriegies who had come to see for themselves what was going on. Within 24 hours, the first of the frontline Red Army troops appeared.

The events of the next few days are predominantly a blur, and the details of specific incidents have merged over time, but my overriding memory is one of intense frustration and excitement in equal measure. It was also a very busy time to be an interpreter and my services were much in demand.

Orders were posted that made it clear that by command of the Soviet military authorities, no one was to either leave or enter the camp. The senior officer in each of the compounds was responsible for ensuring these orders were carried out to the letter. Unfortunately, not everybody was inclined to obey. The difficulty was in several parts. On the one hand, we had the mix of nationalities, and our cultural differences became more obvious and exaggerated as the days went by. Then there was the 'them and us' between officers and NCOs. It has to be remembered that very few of the NCOs were 'regular' RAF, especially among those who had been shot down more recently. A good number had been in the forces for a year or two at most, and for some the initial respect they may have had for their 'superiors' soon turned to suspicion. Who were these officers to prevent them from leaving the camp? Why should they not be allowed to take their chances and flee to the west?

Another difficulty was the sheer volume of prisoners, whose number had been swelled by refugees and other new arrivals, some more welcome than others. German civilians, German army deserters, Red army deserters, local inhabitants, foreign labourers and other POWs all sought refuge in the camp and our protection. Many were turned away, among them the mayor of Luckenwalde who was desperate for us to take his surrender. He had arrived with a large number of women and children in tow, and wanted us to raise the Union Jack above the Rathaus (town hall) so that the Soviets would bypass the town. He was being incredibly naïve, and through me the SBO told him so, at which point the mayor turned nasty, and threatened us with the SS. The SBO was unmoved, and the mayor departed, leaving us with his party of waifs and strays. Everyone, it seemed, wanted to surrender to the West; nobody wanted to be left to the Soviets.

Our Soviet liberators were initially greeted as heroes. They were a tough-looking lot, all battle-hardened and armed to the teeth, and not just men but women too, medical staff, and some of them quite attractive. Half a dozen tanks and other vehicles entered the camp on that first day of liberation, tearing up the main gate and the fence posts that held the barbed wire in check to much cheering and shouting from the prisoners. Some of the Soviets had expensive carpets and silks tied to their vehicles, and other booty that they had evidently looted during their advance, and to which they felt entitled. Vodka was in plentiful supply and shared liberally among us, but food was more of an issue. I ate frozen potatoes and plum jam, an odd combination but when you are close to starving you find that you will eat anything that is put in front of you.

The fighting in the surrounding woods continued, and we could hear small-arms fire and mortars throughout the day. There was considerable fighter activity above our heads, and on one occasion an enemy Junkers 88 swept over the camp and started strafing anything in its path. It was a miracle that nobody was hurt. The Soviets did not want to stay long, and implored us to join them to defeat the enemy. Most of us were too weak to walk more than 50 yards without being out of breath, let alone march and fight with a pack and rifle. Not surprisingly, we declined their invitation, although many of the Soviet prisoners left with them, no doubt keen to display their loyalty to their leader who had condemned all Soviet army prisoners as cowards and traitors.

The frontline troops were soon after replaced by a more permanent Soviet administration under the command of General Fomin, a Guards officer who was formally in charge of the repatriation of POWs in the area. (I believe his actual title was head of the commission for the repatriation of former Allied prisoners of war.) Fomin was a splendid bureaucrat, and I understood both his personality and his role. I recall specifically that around his neck he wore a 'stamp', and unless an order carried his stamp, then nothing would happen that was within his jurisdiction. In the RAF it was commonplace for a junior officer – the adjutant or flight commander – to sign 'on behalf of' the senior officer. Such a thing would have been unthinkable in the Soviet military, and is just one of many differences that existed between our two armed forces.

Foraging parties were established to hunt for food in the surrounding countryside, though this could be a dangerous occupation with the Germans still refusing to surrender and the Red Army prepared to shoot first and ask questions later. (They almost killed one of our Norwegian officers, simply because they did not recognise his uniform as an ally.) The food situation became critical, but through our own endeavours and the help of our new Soviet friends the situation steadily improved.

The following figures are quoted as supplies received in the camp for the whole period April 24 – April 26 inclusive: 9,015 loaves of bread; Pork – 95kg and 82 sides of pork; seven head of cattle; four tons of potatoes; 854kg of beef and beef tallow; 1,850kg of butter; 150kg of onions; 3,000kg of flour; 5,375kg of corn meal and wheat; 625kg of salt; 626kg of pudding powder; 150kg of soup powder; 15,700kg of dried vegetables for soup; 6,000kg of sugar.

A rather attractive Russian woman lieutenant doctor arrived late one evening and wanted details of all of our sick by 0600 hours the following morning. There were at that time 215 seriously ill, 177 other patients confined to bed and 881 other patients registered on sick parade, making 1,273 in all and of all nationalities. Hopes were raised that this might be a sign that our movement was imminent. (I remember the doctor well. On one occasion I was asked to accompany her as interpreter to a meeting outside of the camp grounds. As we drove, we passed a column of German wounded, begging for help. I asked her why we didn't stop. "As a woman," she said, "I'd like to. As a doctor, I must. But as a Soviet officer, they can go to the devil.")

A pass system was put in place without which prisoners could neither leave nor enter the camp, and a further order issued reminding prisoners that anyone caught inside or outside the camp without permission would effectively forfeit the protection of the SBO. It was not an order that was given lightly. A number of airmen had been shot for being in the wrong place at the wrong time, and four French prisoners were gunned down having been found in the town in the company of four women.

The danger was still very real. Dickie created a local 'police' force and picket to maintain order. A Soviet lieutenant colonel paying a social call to the senior allied officer said that there were an estimated 15,000 German troops still loose within a 16-mile radius of the town, wandering about in disorganised bands with the hope of fleeing to the west. None of them wanted to end up in the hands of the Red Army. One of our chaps opted to take off on his own and stumbled into a group about five miles distant, and was lucky to talk his way clear.

General Fomin was at first angry at what he saw as a lack of discipline within the camp. He clearly did not understand the depth of feeling and frustration among the men now in his charge, or why they would want to leave the comparative safety of the group. Collard explained that not all of the men that the general had encountered in the immediate area were from Luckenwalde, and that rather the area was fast becoming the focal point for every waif and stray not already in Soviet hands. Dickie asked how long it would be until we were repatriated. Fomin was pessimistic: whilst it was only his personal view, he did not think there was any immediate prospect of us being sent home, neither could he confirm through which route we would be sent. To us it was simple: it should be to the west; the Soviets, however, had other ideas, and specifically that we would be repatriated via Odessa. This had been agreed previously, and they had no intention of changing their minds.

Conditions within Luckenwalde had improved considerably since the Germans had left, although the French officers in particular seemed to have no pride or interest in instilling any kind of order and discipline among their own men. Fomin's view was that despite our efforts, he could not allow us to live in such uncomfortable circumstances, and gave orders that we should be moved. He seemed to be genuinely concerned for our welfare. Six miles from Luckenwalde on the road to Jüterbog was the Adolf Hitler Lager, a German officers' rest camp and training school. It had been built and equipped on a most luxurious scale with a sports stadium, showers, baths, officers' club, canteen and even a swimming pool, though we were more concerned about finding water to drink rather than to bathe in. Although the camp had been looted, it was still in a comparatively good state of repair; the fabric of the building was most definitely sound.

The orders were that the RAF prisoners were all to be moved. This led to a number of awkward exchanges. Moving such a large number of men was a logistical nightmare. My task as part in these negotiations was to try to find common ground. Collard knew little or nothing of the Soviet people or psyche. I told him as much as I could about their culture, their way of life and their political system so that he was better informed. Dickie for his part was always extremely polite, and always deferential to others of more senior rank.

The respect that he gave to General Fomin was well-received, and certainly helped in the difficult discussions that followed. I explained to the general that we were not in any way resisting the Soviet's intention to move us, but we were anxious that any move might further delay our repatriation.

We were also anxious that the new camp was not a recognised prisoner of war camp, and we did not want, therefore, to be lost from sight from our respective authorities. All of this was true but we had other concerns. Dickie was worried that moving to a new camp would suggest a sense of 'permanency'. This would allow the Soviets an excuse to hold onto us for longer. While we remained at Luckenwalde we could better argue our case that the camp was uninhabitable.

Our principal contact with the outside world was through the BBC, but the news of Germany's imminent collapse only served to fuel our frustrations. German prisoners were seen in their thousands – a mixed group of garrison troops, Luftwaffe men and SS – and they looked a particularly sorry sight. Many were wounded. Four Ukrainian girls arrived in the camp and we listened to their first-hand testimony as to the brutality of their German captors. They had been taken from their homes at 14 and forced to work in an ammunition factory. Later they had been moved to a concentration camp, stripped naked and humiliated in the street by a German doctor who passed the healthy as fit to work while the sick were taken to the gas chambers. They described what went on in the camps: the guards carried cat-of-nine tails, and beatings were a matter of course, the female guards being more brutal than their male colleagues. Kicked and starved, they reported a case of a woman who broke a pane of glass, leading to her entire block of 150 women being given 25 lashes each.

The girls continued to work 12-hour shifts in various factories and were at Torgau when the approach of the Americans led to their evacuation. They travelled in locked cattle trucks, the doors only opened briefly once per day. They were given less than a tenth of a loaf of bread to eat each and hardly any water. The conditions were inhumane. One night while the trucks stood in the New Stettin railway yards sandwiched between two other trains carrying ammunition and fuel, the sidings were bombed. In the explosions that followed, out of the 68 girls in one of the trucks, only five of them escaped. They fled into nearby woods and were hidden in a foreign workers' camp until the Red Army arrived. We had known, of course, that such concentration camps existed, but here for the first time was evidence of the hell to which these people had been subjected.

A rumour was heard around the camp that Hitler was dead. Then it was confirmed. I thought back to my days as a child, as a Jew in Berlin, rejected from joining the Hitler Youth. And of the handshake with my friend at school in England on the day war had been declared. We had come so far. I was alive. But again the joy was short-lived. Hopes were raised again when on May 3, the BBC mentioned Luckenwalde for the first time in one of its reports. We learned that in the past few days, more than 180,000 German soldiers had been killed or captured, including no fewer than seven generals. The situation was now changing by the hour.

A new development that caused a stir was the arrival of two US war correspondents, Bob Vermillion of the United Press and Louis Azreal[25] of the Baltimore News-Post. At last we are able to hear the true situation on the frontline, and why the Americans had not as yet been able to reach us. They had agreed to halt at the Elbe. Unconditional surrender could only be a matter of days away. Another United Press correspondent, Captain Edward Beattie, was returning with his two colleagues and took with him a nominal roll and all information about our present situation and experiences of the previous two weeks. While Beattie was with us he asked if I could help to translate. I agreed on condition that he called my fiancée Jean in Bournemouth to say that I was alive. Later, and much to my surprise, he did. It was the first news she had heard from me in almost six months.

A convoy of US army ambulances arrived on May 5 to evacuate the bulk of the US, British and Norwegian sick. Two lorry loads of bread and two of K rations also arrived. A further convoy was also expected the following day, and the mood in the camp overnight was one of real excitement. Keeping a lid on this was an exacting challenge for our SBO, so much so that he felt obliged to issue a statement to be read out to all officers under his command. The statement, dated May 6 and timed at 1300 hours is worth repeating, for it captures precisely the atmosphere in the camp at that time:

> 'There is a certain atmosphere of flap and excitement among some sections of British officers, which is altogether deplorable and unworthy. I can assure you that you and all British NCOs and other ranks are to be evacuated very shortly to the American lines. I cannot say at present how long the operation will take, but I expect it at least to start today. Meanwhile our food supply here, which has given me great anxiety recently, is for the present assured.

> 'There may have been some slight differences between myself and the Russian authorities here on matters of detail that has been due to the distance from and lack of communications with their own headquarters.

---

25 Azreal had started his career at the age of 16 as a reporter with the *Baltimore Sun*. In 1949, Eisenhower awarded Azreal the Medal of Freedom for his work in covering the war in Europe. He died in 1981 at the age of 77.

'It has simply been a matter of red tape. Let there be an end of the stupid and hysterical speculation and rumour mongering. A British officer commands respect everywhere in Europe, both among our Allies and enemies, and nobody can touch him. See that you are worthy of the complete and universal protection which our flag gives you, and behave with the proper dignity which your reputation demands.'

The 'slight differences' to which the SBO referred were just about to explode into a full-blown row.

It started just two hours after the SBO's statement had been issued. An American jeep, festooned with the stars and stripes, announced its arrival in the camp with a screech of brakes and a cloud of dirt. A convoy of trucks would be arriving within the next few hours and we were to be ready to move out at a moment's notice. This was the news we had all been waiting for. Finally we were going home. Unfortunately, no-one had thought to tell the Soviets.

The first 20 or so trucks pushed through into the camp to begin the evacuation, and small parties of Americans began leaving with what little possessions they still had between them. We were to be evacuated too, along with the Norwegians, French and Belgians in that order. More trucks arrived and then the trouble started. The Americans did not have official permission to evacuate their own men, let alone anyone else, and our Soviet allies made this point clear in the most forceful way possible, by letting off a stream of machine-gun fire over our heads. There was some fast talking on all sides as we tried to prevent a misunderstanding from becoming a massacre.

The Americans had overreached themselves and their authority. They had also overlooked the fact that they were essentially now on Soviet soil, and the Red Army could determine who was allowed in and who was allowed out. The mood in the camp that evening was sombre indeed, for many felt we had simply exchanged one set of guards for another. The senior officer was obliged to issue another statement, stressing that the mix up had been one of procedure and nothing more:

'I have just come back from a conference with the local Russian authorities at which I did my best to demonstrate to them the utter stupidity of delaying our evacuation… the explanation that they offered to me, with profuse apologies, was that on their side, no order to hand us over to the Americans had yet been received. They were confident that such an order would be through shortly, but until it arrived, they would not take the responsibility of letting us go in an unofficial manner. My emphatic argument that the convoy would never have arrived here had it not been officially fixed up, failed to convince them.'

In the conference that Dickie describes, he did indeed warn our Soviet hosts that they were creating a situation that was both serious and ridiculous, and needed to be cleared up quickly. He sent two comparatively senior officers, a wing commander and flight lieutenant, with the Americans to watch our interests at US headquarters, and to plead our case.

This ludicrous game of East-West politics was not quickly resolved and again the Soviets refused to evacuate the RAF. The next day more lorries arrived, but once more the Red Army soldiers steadfastly refused their exit. On that same day, May 7, the last of the Norwegian officers in the camp received orders that they were to depart to the east on the first stage of their repatriation, and that the journey was to be made on foot. This caused quite an argument between the Soviets and General Ruge, and I was called in to intervene.

Now the Norwegian officers always took great pride in their appearance and were always immaculately attired, even to the point of wearing their medals and not just their medal ribbons. Ruge was infuriated at the prospect of being sent home via Odessa, which I believe was the plan, and started to argue with the Red Army general. Quickly I said to him to shout out something in English (the words were not important), tear the medals from his chest, and throw them down in disgust. Ruge did exactly that, throwing them to the floor and muttering something nonsense that I then 'translated'. "The general says that he now places himself and his officers as a prisoner of the Soviets."

Of course Ruge had said nothing of the sort but the Soviet general was not to know that. He stood aghast as Ruge did an about turn and left the meeting. Within the hour, a Red Army major had returned the medals to the Norwegian, with an abject apology, but they would not budge on the orders they had been given. I continued to argue our general's case, and said that the Norwegians' repatriation should be through the usual channels, and that Fomin should say so to his superiors. Fomin smiled when he said to me without humour: "In the Red Army, channels go down from marshals, not up."

In the event the Norwegians were evacuated on May 9. Of the 1,044 Norwegian personnel then still in residence, 806 left the camp that night and into the early morning of May 10. Some 238 stayed behind, mostly the sick or those aged over 55. Their destination at that time was believed to have been Schwiebus and then via cattle trucks to Murmansk and then by ship to Oslo, a journey of some 3,000 miles. A week later and they were still being held in a camp at Liegnitz.

There was another, rather more amusing incident about this time when the Soviets were trying to take a roll call. Three Ukrainian women were in charge of a count that threatened to go on for an interminable time as they attempted to take names and places of birth. Those from London had a comparatively easy time of it, but anyone from Newcastle-upon-Tyne was in for a long wait as the Soviet administrators struggled to understand their accents. Pretty quickly we passed word that everyone was to say that they were from London, regardless of their genuine pedigree. A senior Red Army officer arrived and became suspicious, but appeared to believe me when I told him that this was a camp exclusively for Londoners.

There was also another amusing incident involving a Mercedes car. During our various ongoing negotiations we had been obliged to visit the Red Army major who had been placed in charge of the town. His style was brutal and to the point. He would summons the local farmers and tell them how much grain and livestock he needed, and give them 24 hours to deliver or else they would be shot. It was a three-mile walk into town, and given our physical state and the need to see him every day we asked if we might have use of a car. He told us to take our pick of a group of staff cars that had been captured or requisitioned. We chose a rather fine Mercedes and headed back into camp. We had not gone far, however, when we were stopped by a Soviet patrol and ordered to get out of the car. I began to protest, at which point a menacing bayonet was waved in my face and so we did as we were told and walked the rest of the way back into town. We explained what had happened, and the major apologised and told us to take another. He also gave us an official document to explain our business, and to present if we were to run into any more trouble. We did. We were stopped at the same check point, by the same patrol, with the exact same result. On the third occasion, the major lent us one of his officers with a sub-machine gun around his neck. Strange to report we did not seem to have any more trouble after that.

It was to be another two weeks before we were finally set free, and when it happened it was somewhat surreal. We had grown bored and maybe a little irritated with the BBC announcers recounting tales of VE day and the celebrations that had passed us by. Now we were the forgotten many who just wanted to get home and get back to normality – whatever that was. A meeting between the SBO and a Red Army representative for the repatriation of allied officers on May 19 had finally ended in agreement. The exchange of all remaining Anglo-American and Soviet prisoners was to take place at 1200 hours Central European Time on May 20. We were to travel in Red Army lorries from Luckenwalde to Torgau where we would be handed over to the Americans. The Americans, meanwhile, would then exchange their Soviet POWs in a straight swap. We were not allowed to leave the camp, however, until such time as the Soviets had received word that their compatriots had already arrived.

Loading onto the vehicles was yet another farce. I had previously asked how many trucks would be arriving so that I could help organise the prisoners into appropriately-sized groups and so speed our departure. The Soviets refused to give me such information, telling me that it was a military secret. When the lorries did finally arrive, we had to move along the convoy as one enormous group, detaching prisoners at intervals to clamber onboard. By the time we arrived at the head of the convoy and the last lorry, we obviously still had too many men and so had to decant them in one's and two's in the trucks that were already full. Then, just as we were about to leave, a party of Soviet soldiers arrived carrying sacks of grain and flower, and driving a number of heads of cattle. They ordered the prisoners off the first three lorries in order to load the provisions. I tried to argue that we could do without, but the agreement was that the prisoners of war in their charge should be properly provisioned, and so they were going to stick to their agreement. It was the Soviet way.

When we at last departed, the journey was long and tortuous, but accompanied by an enormous sense of anticlimax. Having waited so long for freedom, now it had finally arrived it did not seem somehow real. We spent about six hours in those lorries, journeying across the wasteland of Nazi Germany. All around us were the signs of battle, of death and decay, smashed buildings, vehicles and men. It seemed remarkable that the defeat of the once almighty German armies could have been so devastatingly complete.

We arrived at the Elbe, by the pontoon that had been renamed 'The Bridge of Friendship' where the US and Soviet military had met for the first time, and the propaganda people had witnessed their finest hour. The colonel in charge of the US convoy greeted us with much warmth but his good humour soon turned to anger when the Red Army officer in charge demanded that he personally sign for every prisoner in his charge. The colonel of course was furious, and the boys started getting restless. Even at this eleventh hour we were to be held back by bureaucracy and red tape.

The Soviets set out a table on which was placed the nominal roll. Our men (who had by now all clambered down from their trucks) queued in an orderly fashion and as they stated their names, they had to wait for their name to be found, one by one. Of course we all quickly realised that this process was going to take all day and half the night, and so I happened upon an idea. Since I could see the list to read it, I whispered the next name on the list to the next man in the queue. That speeded things up considerably, and if the Soviets in charge appreciated the happy coincidence he was equally happy to keep quiet. It was not for him to validate the true identity of each man. All he required was a signature, and he got it.

In the event we spent some three or four days at Halle, billeted in accommodation that had once been occupied by Luftwaffe aircrew, before being flown by Dakota to Brussels where we were given a 24-hour pass. Few of us felt like celebrating. From Brussels we were ultimately flown by Lancaster back to the UK, and thence on to RAF Cosford to be processed (My papers say that I was posted to 106 Personnel Reception Centre as from May 25.)

We were 'de-briefed' on our experiences, and subjected to a series of medical examinations to check on our general health and well-being. I had only been a prisoner for a comparatively short period of time and was still relatively fit, but those who had been behind barbed wire for three, four and sometimes five years or more suffered from all manner of ailments brought on by poor diet.

I was not kept too long, however, and when fully recovered I was given a new uniform, money, a travel voucher and a copy of the *Daily Mirror*. I was also given an envelope that I opened to find a summons for driving without registration or insurance, from the incident with the policeman in Beverley, a lifetime ago. It was accompanied by two further letters, one from the RAF to the magistrate saying that I had been killed in action and another from the magistrate expressing sympathy for my loss. I felt reports of my death had been somewhat over-exaggerated.

CHAPTER FIVE

FINDING MY WAY

It was for me, like every returning serviceman or Kriegie, an emotional if somewhat confusing time, and one that required a period of re-adjustment. I had been absent for a little over a year, a relatively short period compared to some of my fellow prisoners, but even in 12 months a great deal had changed.

On July 7, 1945 Jean and I were married in church in Bournemouth. This had been made possible courtesy of Jean's grandmother who liked me very much. She had wanted for us to be married in church, despite my faith, and arranged for us to meet a senior Church of England official in Winchester to see what could be done. He asked me if I believed in God, and my answer was sufficient that he said that if he was able to create a service where there was no mention of the mother of God, the holy trinity or Jesus Christ – and there was no genuflecting – would I be happy to be married in church? I was indeed happy, and so our unique service was conducted to everyone's satisfaction. I cannot think of any other country or religion in the world that would have been so accommodating.

We spent our honeymoon in London staying at the Waldorf. One evening we were invited to a party across the road and I refused to walk, demanding that we took a taxi instead. I had rather had my fill of walking. Nine months later our first child, Carol Anne, was born. Three more would follow in due course: Julian (named after my father on January 14, 1950); Tanya (October 24, 1951); and the youngest, Paul (September 25, 1953).

I had further good news soon after when a small, brown package arrived for me in the post. I opened it with some bemusement to see that it contained a group of medals, sent to me from the Air Ministry 'for services rendered'. They included an aircrew Europe Star. A little while later I received another medal in the post that I was not familiar with, a foreign decoration from the King of Norway. It transpired I had been awarded the Norwegian Cross of Liberty, as had Dickie Collard, for our support of General Ruge and his people in the camps. It was really a very great surprise and honour to be so recognised. All foreign decorations had to be approved by the British authorities, and I felt I was still only a young man to be granted such a high reward. On reflection I felt I deserved it, but it was rather more of a surprise to find out that other people thought so too. (As an amusing aide-memoire, whenever I met Dickie at various RAF reunions or gatherings after the war, he would always invite me to his table to the bemusement of those other senior officers around him. They could never understand why a group captain would have such a close relationship with a mere warrant officer.)

By now news had reached me that my mother was alive and in Naples. She was refusing to return from Italy until she knew what had happened to me. The authorities, however, said that unless she found a job, she would be obliged to leave, and so she secured a post as an official in the International Red Cross. Since I was in London, and was near the Air Ministry, Jean suggested I went in and enquired whether something could be done. I can criticise the Royal Air Force for many things, but the speed with which they addressed the issue of my mother was commendable. Within five or ten minutes of explaining my predicament to a young WAAF, I was called in to the office of a squadron leader (medical officer) and repeated my story. I had to go a little way to convince him I was not totally mad, but he said he would look into it and I was to be patient.

In the event I did not have to wait long, and within 48 hours I was on my way to Naples in yet another Dakota. When the aircraft landed I was met by a jeep. The US Army driver said that he had been instructed to drive me to the hotel where my mother had been staying. It was an anxious moment as the receptionist called my mother's room and I waited for her to come down. I had not seen her for six years. The lift in the hotel opened out into the lobby, and it was an emotional moment when I saw the lift doors open and my mother emerge. She looked me up and down and said simply: "If I had had my way you would have gone to Oxford and never have joined the RAF." My mother was nothing if not honest. Then she burst into tears.

I had not told my mother I was coming and in the event spent about a fortnight in Naples. The war had been incredibly difficult for her and she had survived through a combination of luck, guile, and dogged determination. My father had not been so lucky. The Jews in Poland had all been systematically eliminated. Once identified, he had been obliged to wear the Star of David on his coat to mark him out as a Jew. Then he had been forced to live in the Warsaw Ghetto, where hundreds of men, women and children died every day from starvation, hyperthermia and all manner of ailments and diseases that pervaded the city. My mother, who lived separately, used what few items of jewellery she still had left (she had the foresight to escape with them) to buy food and have it smuggled in – a risky operation that could have easily resulted in her own arrest. Then one day, my father wasn't there.

It was a rule that if a Jew was on the pavement, and approached by a German soldier, he was to step into the gutter to make way. One day, I learned, my father had been on the pavement and had refused to step aside. He had been immediately arrested, probably beaten and certainly transported. He is one of the countless thousands who simply disappeared and was never heard of again. I believe he was sent to the death camp at Treblinka, and perhaps regret that I did not do more at the time to find out for certain. On the memorial that stands at the railway station from which the Jews were sent on their final journey, the first names of the innocent have been recorded. Among those names is one that matches my father's. I know that I am incredibly proud of the stand that he made. It fits with my memory of the man.

While I was away, Jean stayed in Bournemouth, and during my absence the RAF Police came to her house and demanded to know where I was. I had been 'lost' in the system and listed as a deserter. They were, I'm afraid, rather aggressive but Jean gave as good as she got and sent them on their way having satisfied their enquiries. After I returned to the UK, however, I had a touch of sandfly fever and was put into a Canadian air force hospital in Bournemouth. Here I was once again 'lost' and once again reported as a deserter for the second time in as many weeks. Happily this situation was also quickly resolved. I was still in the RAF and therefore subject to their discipline and laws.

So now came the tricky problem of what to do with me. Demobilisation (demob) was taking its time, and I wasn't exactly high on the RAF's list of the most deserving cases. The first job they offered me was as a physical training instructor (PTI). How they arrived at that decision I will never know, for a person more unlike a PTI it is difficult to imagine. Then they offered me a job working in charge of stores at a remote airfield in the north of Scotland. This was typical air force. I could not have possibly been of any use in Scotland, whereas my skills in speaking fluent German and Russian appeared to have been completely overlooked. It would also mean that I would be several hundreds of miles away from my new wife. Fortunately, and after making my position very clear, a different post was offered to me – in Berlin. Notwithstanding I would again be parted from Jean, the role, as an intelligence officer, was at least better matched to my talents.

To be back in Berlin after so many years was a strange and rather disorientating experience. It had changed so much and yet it had not changed at all. Of course the destruction caused by the Allied bombing and the Soviet army had been catastrophic, but enough of the city had survived to retain its underlying character. One of my first jobs was to drive around with a corporal that I had been allocated, making sure that all of the swastikas were removed from the public buildings. We were instructed that anyone who refused would be locked up.

I visited the house that I had lived in as a child before being forced out by the Nazis, and the school where I had been educated. I remember a joke that was going around at the time about a Jew travelling on a tram through the city, and the German tram conductor announcing the various stops: 'Berlin Square, formerly Adolf Hitler Square. The Brandenburg Gate, formerly Adolf Hitler Gate etc. When it came to his stop, the Jew thanked the conductor to which the conductor replied: "Not at all comrade, formerly a yid."

As part of my intelligence posting I was attached to an RAF disarmament unit, a unit set up to assess German weaponry and equipment to see what we could learn from it. This was much at the same time as both the Americans and the Soviets were searching for German scientists to gain an advantage at the very start of the space and nuclear race.

There was one particular story worth recounting. A RAF pilot, ostensibly on a 'training flight' near the Russian sector had found himself in trouble and was obliged to crash-land. The Spitfire came down in the Russian zone and the pilot was happily unharmed. But while the Soviets allowed the pilot to return, they would not allow the RAF to recover their aircraft. And so there was an impasse. However much the British claimed the pilot was simply a novice who had become lost, the Soviets were adamant he was a spy. A few days later, however, a Soviet pilot found himself in much the same predicament, coming down with his aircraft in the British sector. Since the Soviets had refused to return our aircraft, the British authorities did the same, and so an exchange was arranged, with me in charge of the exchange party.

The meeting to discuss the exchange was a memorable affair. Indeed it wasn't just the one meeting, but rather the discussions went on for several days. We met in a large room that was packed with Red Army officers. I spoke first, sticking to the story that the pilot was an innocent man who had lost his way, and that as former allies, they had a duty to return our aircraft to us. The Soviets refused. We could not have the aircraft back, and they would broach no further discussion on the matter. With that, the meeting came to an end and we had lunch, dining on the very best caviar, vodka and champagne. The meeting reconvened in the afternoon and I started again with my entreaties. They, once again, refused. And so this charade went on for three days. The sergeant who had accompanied me spent the entire time doing his crossword.

On the third day, after I had made the same request and listened to the same speech in reply, another Soviet officer walked in. There was a whispered exchange with his fellow officers and then a pronouncement was made. Although the lead negotiator went through his entire preamble (which by now we could all of us recite verbatim), the honourable Soviet military had given their consent. We were given a map, and a route to follow. Indeed they could not have done more to help us find our downed aircraft. For our part, we gave them a bottle of Scotch.

We drove out in a convoy comprising a jeep, several lorries and a Queen Mary transporter, so named because of its enormous size. A Queen Mary was the standard road-based aircraft transporter (the lorries have changed little in the last 50 years), with a crane attached for lifting damaged aircraft onto its back. Several comedy moments happened on that trip. For one, the crane protruding from the lorry managed to swing loose and get itself entangled with one of the enormous portraits of Stalin that had sprung up all over the city, and pulled the whole thing down. This proved embarrassing, but fortunately for us, no action was taken.

Along the route all was going well until we came upon a party of Soviet troops standing across the road (this is the Russians' method of hitchhiking). We stopped, not that we had much of a choice, and a young officer approached. He told us that we were not to go any further, and that we must follow him and his men. At this point I started to argue. I said that we had a map and clear instructions of where we were to be and when. It was vital that we kept to the Soviet schedule we had been given, for that was the only way we could ensure safe passage. The officer demanded that we handed over our weapons (we all carried sidearms) and I refused. "I would not surrender my weapons to the enemy," I told him, "and I am certainly not going to surrender them to my allies."

It seemed to do the trick. Although we were allowed to keep our weapons, we could not carry on with our journey and went in convoy to a small town that was somewhat out of our way. Despite my bravado about our weapons (remember I was only 22), it was now getting more

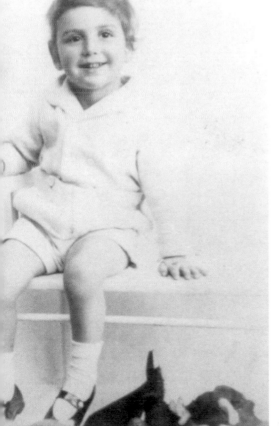

Above left: Andy's mother, Stella Weizman.
Above right: Andy and his father, Julian Weizman.
Left: Andy as a toddler.

Top left: Andy and Jean.
Top right: Andy's wife, Jean.
Above: Andy's children, from left to right; Julian, Tanya, Paul and Carol Anne.
Opposite top left: Andy's mother and father in a society shot.
Opposite top right: What the posh kids were wearing.
Opposite bottom: Andy with his father.

Top: Course photograph of 9 ITW.
Above left: Andy at ITW. Note the Polish shoulder flash can just be seen.
Above right: Andy in flying overalls.

Opposite top left: Flight Sergeant Barry Casey.
Opposite top right: Sergeant Abbott Camp.
Opposite bottom: The graves of Flight Sergeants Swan, Casey and Lyall at Poix-de-la-Somme (now known as Poix-de-Picardie).

Top left: A Halifax of 466 Squadron, similar to the aircraft in which Andy was shot down.
Middle left: Halifax MZ296 lands with its port outer cut.
Below: A happy group of warrant officers and NCOs outside 'The Bristol' NAAFI. Andy is second from right.
Opposite left: Andy and a friend take a break from training.
Opposite right: Formal portrait of Andy Wiseman.
Opposite bottom: Alcohol and cigarettes were in plentiful supply in the warrant officers' mess.

Top left: Allied bombing had reduced large swathes of Germany to rubble.
Top right: Andy as a Kriegie – his official POW identity photograph.
Above: A photograph of the railway marshalling yards at Tergnier. This was Andy's target on the night he failed to return.

than a little scary. We were taken to a room and given some food. I tried to frighten the Soviet officer by telling him that I was there with the authority of General Zhukov, and that when he found out that we had been effectively 'kidnapped', they would no doubt all be shot.

We spent a nervous few hours in that room until at last the Soviet officer entered and said to me that it had all been a mistake. We were indeed authorised to continue our journey but nobody had thought to tell him as an officer commanding the local area. He knew that in preventing us from travelling, he might have been shot; but he also knew that had he allowed an RAF convoy through that did not have the correct authority, he would definitely have been shot. The next morning, after an enjoyable evening where the vodka flowed, he escorted us back to the exact spot that we had been taken so that we could continue our onward journey.

Our adventures, however, were far from over. We arrived in a small town near to where the Spitfire had crashed and were taken to the site – a field that was guarded by two Soviet soldiers. They had been there for weeks, taking turns to stand guard and sleep in a makeshift hut. The aircraft looked rather forlorn, with its nose sticking into the ground and its tail pointing in the air. The local Soviet army officers were very correct and wanted to do everything by the book. I was asked to confirm that none of the petrol, for example, had been siphoned from the tanks. I did not have a clue, neither did I especially care, but thankfully my sergeant was rather more practical and fashioned a dipstick out of a twig and confirmed that everything was how it should be. They then set about the substantial task of lifting the aircraft from its resting place and onto the back of the transporter.

With the heavy lifting completed we drove to a nearby hotel where we would stay the night before returning home the next morning. While we were there, my sergeant struck up a conversation with a local German woman, at which point he was rounded upon by our Soviet hosts. Our liaison officer told us in no uncertain terms that we were not to fraternise with German women, and we were certainly not allowed to speak to them. Rather chastened, we did as we were told and nothing more was said on the matter. I went off to dine in the Soviet officers' mess and by the time I got back to the hotel it was already morning. I was drunk, but not so drunk that I did not recognise my sergeant sitting in the lobby.

"What are you doing here?" I asked.

"When I got to my room, there was a naked woman lying in my bed," he replied.

"What did you do?"

"I didn't do anything. You said we could not fraternise so I have spent the whole night down here waiting for you."

We went up to my room where I slept on my bed and he slept on the floor – shades of me and Dickie at Luckenwalde. The story became funnier just before it was time to leave. Our Soviet liaison officer sidled up to me and asked me (using internationally-recognised finger gestures) whether my sergeant had spent an enjoyable night with the woman he had arranged for him. I told him no because we had been told not to fraternise. "Ah," he replied, "what we say in public is different to what we do in private."

Our excursion to recover the Spitfire was one of the highlights of my brief tour of duty in Intelligence in Bad Eilsen. Another was my brief part in tracking down a Gestapo officer responsible for murdering one of 'the fifty'. Although I was in Germany because of my language skills, I was not actually part of the official interpreters unit that had been set up many months earlier while I was still a prisoner of war. That did not mean, however, that my services were not required, and I was occasionally called upon to help out. One such occasion was when I was sent for by Squadron Leader Frank McKenna, a former policeman who was heading up the hunt for the men who had murdered Squadron Leader Roger Bushell and the other 49 POWs shot following the Great Escape. Having been in Stalag Luft III and seen the impact of the murders on the surviving Kriegies first hand, I was only too keen to help.

We travelled to a small town not far from Hamburg to an address where one of the Gestapo men was believed to be living. We banged on the door and it was opened by a middle-aged German woman. She was immediately suspicious. I told her who we were and that we were looking for her husband. Despite some forthright questioning, she insisted that she did not know where he was and it soon became clear that short of beating it out of her, she was not going to alter her story. Before we left, however, I said that if she ever changed her mind, or suddenly remembered where her husband was, that she could get in touch, and gave her an address at which I could be reached. At that we departed, with the woman still standing at the door as we drove away.

About a fortnight later, I did indeed receive a letter to say that she wanted to meet. We jumped into a jeep to see her and she gave me a note with her husband's new name (he was hiding under an alias) and address. I was somewhat surprised at her change of heart, and asked her why she had not said anything during our previous visit. She said to me coldly, that two weeks ago she did not know that he was playing around with a young girl, and that she had been spurned. We went to the address she had given us, and the man was arrested. Hell, it seems, does indeed have no fury like a woman scorned.

There was another more light-hearted occasion when I was called to see Sir William Sholto Douglas, one of our more prominent wartime commanders who had for a time been in charge of Fighter Command. There was a Czech RAF Spitfire squadron stationed near Prague that was running short of aviation fuel, and the Soviets were being awkward with regards facilitating further supplies. I was asked to go along with a convoy of fuel, commanded by a flight lieutenant, and act an interpreter. Despite the air marshal's exalted position, I had the courage to point out that I spoke no Czech.

"But," he said to me, "your file says that you are an interpreter."

"That is true," I replied, and had the temerity to add: "But I hope you would never send me to China."

At this point he ended the conversation: "If I order you to go to China to interpret, you will go to China to interpret."

The air marshal had the last laugh. When I got to Prague, I quickly discovered that everybody spoke either Russian or German.

Not long after, a chance meeting was to have a profound effect on the rest of my life. I was driving through Berlin when a jeep overtook me and then fell behind. It overtook me again, and then once again fell behind at which point the driver started flashing his headlights – a universal signal to stop. I dutifully pulled over and a man in uniform stepped out and approached. He was about ten years older than me and seemed vaguely familiar, but I could not place him, at least not immediately. He asked me if I was André, to which I replied I was, and then I recognised him as Alexander Elkin, the son of a couple that my parents had known as friends before the war. They had been part of a large group of Russian émigrés with whom my mother and father had socialised in Berlin.

It was a happy reunion on many fronts, and we arranged to go for a drink and talk some more. Elkin, it transpired, had spent the war as a monitor at the BBC, listening in on radio broadcasts and providing transcripts of conversations to assess for intelligence and news-gathering purposes. He was currently working for an economic organisation in Paris. He asked me what I intended to do, now that the war was over, and I told him honestly that I didn't have much of an idea. He asked whether I might be interested in working for the BBC. He thought I might be suitable and gave me an address to write to. After that, it was down to me.

The more I thought about the idea, the more it appealed. I wrote to the BBC and a few weeks later they invited me for tests and an interview in London. This was obviously a little bit awkward as I was still 'employed' by the RAF so I asked my CO for help. He pulled strings, though what I had done to deserve it I am not quite sure, and a few weeks later I was on my way to England (once again in a Dakota).

The process was extremely thorough and took two days of tests and interviews. This included an intelligence test, and being quizzed on my knowledge of languages. They did this by playing recordings of radio broadcasts from Moscow, Warsaw and Berlin and asking me to translate. These were not crystal clear transmissions, it should be understood, which added an extra layer of complexity, but I still managed without difficulty. Happily I passed with flying colours and they offered me a job. On returning to my unit in Germany, I went to tell my CO the happy news and he seemed genuinely pleased for me, so pleased that he arranged for my demob to become official one month after my new job had started. And so I found myself in the unusual situation of starting at the BBC whilst still being officially employed by the RAF – at least for a few weeks.

The history of monitoring radio broadcasts can actually be traced to the First World War when the Home Secretary instructed Scotland Yard to form a special department to listen in to German radio broadcasts. The 'programmes' at the time comprised a combination of music and talks broadcast to troops on the western front by the man described as 'the father of German broadcasting' – Hans Bredow. The department really came to prominence in the 1930s, when the Foreign Office began monitoring English-language news bulletins from Italy, specifically to learn more about Il Duce's progress in his war in Abyssinia. Monitoring of Arabic broadcasts from Italy followed in 1937, and programmes transmitted from Germany to South America attracted the attention of the Foreign Office the following year. Most of the monitoring was undertaken by the then BBC Receiving Station at Tatsfield, although the Foreign Office also had a site at Sandridge near St Albans. Both had circuits to Broadcasting House in London.

By this time, the BBC had itself begun broadcasting to an overseas audience via what it called the Empire Service, covering primarily the Near East and Middle East. It was soon recognised in London, however,

that listening to indigenous programmes would provide useful content for
the BBC's own transmissions. As such, by the end of 1938 the 'listeners' at
Tatsfield were monitoring news bulletins from several European countries
as well as Tokyo and New York. With war looming, it was decided in April
1939 that a dedicated monitoring unit should be established, its function
being to provide content both for the BBC news programmes and to the
newly formed Ministry of Information, although the latter declined to
contribute to its financing[26].

Early in the war the Monitoring Unit moved from London to Wood Norton,
near Evesham, occupying a site more reminiscent of a prisoner of war camp
than a high-tech listening service, with staff working from an odd assortment
of wooden huts. From a technical perspective, two teleprinter circuits linked
the unit to the BBC News department and the MOI. It performed well,
providing round the clock monitoring of all forms of broadcast transmissions
in voice, Morse and even teleprinter. As the volumes of broadcasts increased,
so too did the numbers of monitors. By 1943 it was clear that the scope
for further development at Wood Norton was limited and the unit (now
officially renamed the Monitoring Service) moved to Caversham Park, near
Reading. As well as a large mansion house, which offered far more room than
that available at Wood Norton, 109 acres of land were acquired at the same
time. A second site at Crowsley Park, some three miles from Caversham
Park, was also acquired for use as a receiver site. It was to Caversham Park
that I reported for my first day in what was to be a long and enjoyable career
at the BBC.

The head of the monitors was a Russian prince with the impressive
and grand title of Prince André Beloselsky-Belozersky. His father had been
a celebrated tsarist general who had made England his home. André was a
well-educated, highly-intelligent man who I took to immediately, possibly
because of his loathing for bureaucracy and love of drink. He was also
extremely good-looking, and as a single man, a considerable draw for the
ladies, although I was never sure he was that way inclined. He could certainly
be very charming and amused me with his outlook on life that included the
view that work should only be the prerogative of the working classes.

André was by no means unique; the monitors at Caversham were an

26 Edward Pawley, in his book *BBC Engineering 1922–1972*, writes that the Corporation '…pur-
chased out of its own funds a wooden hut, six receivers and material for simple aerials for the sum
of £810 in the hope of recovering this outlay from the ministry later on.' It is not known whether any
money was indeed recovered.

eclectic and somewhat eccentric bunch from all over Europe. There were Germans, Poles, Russians, Italians, French and Serbo-Croats, including one who had fought in the Spanish Civil War – apparently on the wrong side. The biggest 'teams' were those working on the Russian and German language broadcasts; most of them were refugees and all of them had a fascinating story to tell. I was, to them, somewhat of a curiosity, being the youngest by far and the only one amongst us who had seen action against the Germans, but I quickly felt part of the team.

My task, I learned, was a relatively simple one. In those days, there were no such things as foreign correspondents, at least not in any substantial numbers, and so our role was to listen to open radio broadcasts, translate those broadcasts, and report what was being said. We were therefore part translators and part sub-editors, an early form of multi-tasking. The information that we gathered was fed into a central news bureau, and its content sent by teleprinter to the BBC newsrooms in London, the Foreign Office and other organisations with an interest in what was happening on the European continent. London then used some of this content either as part of, or to better inform, its own broadcasts.

We did not only 'feed' our own BBC, however. Our reports were also compiled into a daily digest and distributed further afield to various subscribers (I believe these digests are still available). Urgent news content was of course prioritised, but the BBC knew how to make capital out of their knowledge from the outset. One incident remains uppermost in my mind even 60 years after the event. We operated a rota system that sometimes meant working through the night, and occasionally on your own. One night I was checking the TASS tape news service (TASS was the Soviet news agency), when I saw that Stalin, the Soviet leader, had suffered a stroke. I rushed into the news bureau to tell the duty editor who that night happened to be Ted Rance, a fellow Kriegie. Instinctively I knew that despite what they were reporting, Stalin was dying. Ted, of course, told me to bugger off out of his office but I insisted and finally he was persuaded that I wasn't joking. I sat with Ted and we continued to watch the Russian tape until shortly afterwards, the Soviet radio station started playing sombre music – almost always presaging bad news.

This was potentially one of the biggest scoops we were ever likely to get at the BBC and we were determined to be first with the news. As such, I had one of the teleprinter girls type out the message 'Stalin Dead. Official' and make it ready to send as soon as his death was confirmed. All of the Soviet radio stations closed down with the exception of one, one that imparted its news to the whole of the USSR in what was known as dictation speed. Then the announcer started:

… Dear comrades and friends: The Central Committee of the Communist Party of the Soviet Union, the USSR, Council of Ministers and the Presidium of the USSR, Supreme Soviet announce with profound sorrow to the party and all workers of the Soviet Union that on the 5th of March, at 2150 hours, after a grave illness….

At this point I risked my career by saying that Stalin was dead before Moscow radio had announced it.

….the Chairman of the USSR. Council of Ministers and the Secretary of the Central Committee of the Communist Party of the Soviet Union…

I then had a momentary panic for a few seconds that it might not be Stalin, but one of the other founding fathers of the Soviet Union, such as Molotov, and that I had potentially just made the biggest mistake of my life before finally the words came out,

….Joseph Vissarionovich Stalin, died.

Never have I been so relieved to hear someone's name announced in relation to a death. While the announcer droned on that 'the heart of the comrade and inspired continuer of Lenin's will… has stopped beating…' the news was being flashed to Broadcasting House and thence on to the various international news agencies: Stalin Dead. Official says BBC. It was most certainly a night to remember.

During my time with the Monitoring Service, my work brought me into contact with the Foreign Broadcast Information Services (FBIS), in effect our US equivalent. This American entity began operations in 1941 along the same lines as the BBC Monitoring Service but as the result of a more directly governmental initiative. As part of the 1948 UK/USA Agreement, the BBC and FBIS agreed to exchange information derived from monitored material and divided the world into areas of interest.

The FBIS had a station on Cyprus and welcomed BBC monitors to achieve a degree of co-operation. Since I was rather bored with Caversham, I was keen to go but there was a snag: Jean was pregnant. To give some idea of the paternal nature of the BBC in those days, they actually came to see

Jean to have her assurance that it was OK for me to go, and that I had not coerced her in any way. It was important to them that it was a joint decision, taken without undue influence.

In Cyprus I was billeted at the Dome Hotel in Kyrenia and enjoyed one of my happiest times, though I did nearly end up with the sack. There was a strict rule while working for the BBC that we were not allowed to speak unofficially to the press, or contribute to their reporting unless it was with the express permission of a higher BBC authority – at least one considerably higher than mine. In my particular hotel there was a journalist called Ian Colvin who had a daily column of 'inside information' that he put together for a national newspaper. Ian made it known that he would pay £5 for any information he received that made it into his column, and a further £10 if that information proved to be true. I saw this as an easy way of making some equally easy money, and so began feeding him such news as came my way. Somehow, however, my little ruse was discovered (so much for the media boast of not revealing your sources) and I found myself summoned by the head of the Monitoring Service (HMS) who happened to be a former RAF officer.

It was clear that I had gone too far and was in serious trouble. It seemed that I might lose my job. Now it should be said, in my defence that I never once gave any information that Ian Colvin's newspaper did not already receive by way of our daily digests, but he obviously couldn't be bothered to read it. I said this to the HMS who asked me with a straight face whether I had ever thought of becoming a barrister.

I should have been immediately suspended, but the Monitoring Service was short of Russian monitors and I was told that the HMS would consider my fate and let me know. I was due to have a knee operation, and on the last afternoon of my last day, my future still hung in the balance. My shift ended at 4p.m. and at 3:55p.m. HMS' secretary Gill came down and told me that the boss wanted to see me at 5:30p.m. As I walked up to his office, I passed André who winked at me and said: "You are just about to believe in the resurrection." He also added: "For God's sake don't go in there smiling!"

Luckily I was not sacked; I simply had to give him my word of honour (whatever that was worth) to promise that it would never happen again, that I would never again speak to the press, and that such a transgression would never be repeated. (A few years after this incident, I met the HMS at a party and he was pleased to hear that I was doing well in my new job in television. I asked him why he hadn't sacked me. His response rather took me aback: "I asked London for advice on what to do with you and they ordered me to sack you," he said. "I told them that I didn't take orders from London about my staff. Had they *advised* me to sack you, then I might well have done." By such fine margins are one's futures decided.

My time at the Monitoring Service was coming to a natural end. I had progressed from being a monitor to working as a sub in the News Bureau, but to me it was clear that television offered more prospects for advancement and so I began scouting for opportunities. The head of the News Bureau, Charles Landon, seemed to quite like me and alerted me to an opportunity as a sub-editor in BBC TV News at Alexandra Palace. The job had been advertised internally, but for some reason I had missed it.

I once had cause to annoy Charles concerning the News Bureau log in which we wrote messages and aide-memoires. Updating the log was especially important when you were on the nightshift or in cases where you might not see your colleagues from one week to the next and there was important news to convey to other members of the team. I wrote an entry in the log in red ink, underneath which Charles had written: '...only heads of department are allowed to use red ink. Are you being aggressive or absent minded...' I wrote two words in red ink: 'absent minded'.

I applied for the post and was delighted to be called for interview, which again consisted of a series of tests in the presence of my new potential boss to ensure I didn't cheat. Once more I seemed to attain sufficient marks to be offered the job, and so with some trepidation but not a little excitement left the comfort of the Monitoring Service for the brave world of television news. It was a decision I never had cause to regret.

CHAPTER SIX

TOMORROW'S WORLD

The story of television is well known. It can trace its roots back almost 150 years, although the world's first public demonstration did not happen until 1926. The BBC's initial engagement with television was somewhat tentative. It reluctantly agreed to transmit television broadcasts, but because it had only one transmitter – and for television you need two – the first broadcasts had to alternate between two minutes of sound and two minutes of picture. Programme making at the BBC began in 1932, but in 1934 the government set up a committee to explore the possibility of a high-definition service with a minimum of 240 lines per picture. Two rival systems were to compete via a London station, that station to be built and operated by the BBC.

Tasked with finding a suitable location that could house studios, sound transmitters, masts and aerials, the BBC alighted upon Alexandra Palace, a rather forlorn and run-down former Victorian entertainments complex in North London that had the good fortune of being perched on a hill. This was essential if the pictures were to be received at a reliable range of up to 25 metres. After considerable hard work, BBC Television formally opened for business on November 2, 1936 with a series of speeches from government representatives.

With the outbreak of war, the transmitter was switched off, and BBC television broadcasts came to an abrupt halt. It was switched on again on June 7, 1946, but any euphoria generated by its return was short-lived. Money was tight, and some began to doubt whether television could survive. There was also considerable snobbery regarding ownership of the news. For many years, the bigwigs at Broadcasting House had deemed that news in vision would be inappropriate – a somewhat ludicrous notion. Those who were heavily entrenched in radio believed that pictures interfered with the news, and the expressions of a newscaster could suggest an emotion or feeling that could be misinterpreted. But eventually common sense prevailed, and in January 1948, a weekly bulletin of filmed reports was launched.

Without doubt the BBC's crowning moment, both literally and metaphorically, came in 1953 with what was recognised at the time as being the most demanding outside broadcast in the (then) brief history of television. It was, of course, the Queen's coronation. The BBC had experimented with outside broadcasts from the outset (outside cameras had been used first to cover the RadiOlympia Exhibition at London's Olympia) but movement of cameras was restricted by the need for a reliable cable link with the studio. In 1937, some eight miles of cable was laid around London for the coronation of King George VI and the broadcast was said to be a triumph.

The BBC now looked to repeat this success with the King's daughter, but it was not without its challenges. Cameras had been banned from covering the King's funeral, and the media speculated on whether they would be banned again from such an intimate royal ceremony. As it was, they need not have worried; the broadcast proved more popular than the BBC could ever have imagined. With transmitters now installed all over the country, more than 18 million people watched the ceremony on their TV screens, either at home or with friends. It proved a triumph, not just in the UK, but also overseas where telerecordings of their coverage were flown to the United States, for example, for more than 85 million Americans to watch.

That year, the manufacture of TV sets outstripped the manufacture of radios for the first time. Thanks largely to the coronation, by 1954 there were more than 3.2 million television sets in use in British homes, and the future of BBC Television was assured. It was into this mix that I arrived to work as a sub on BBC Television News, reporting to the duty editor. My role was a challenging one, working very much at the coal face: I had to take news reports from multiple regional, national and international sources, as well as BBC correspondents, and cut their reports to a news bulletin of not more than one minute and 20 seconds in length.

From the outset I was welcomed as one of the team. The same paternal culture that had existed in my monitoring services days was very much in evidence at Ally Pally, as it came to be known. But that is not to say that there were not the doomsayers who still seemed to believe that television would not last, and that radio was for the intelligentsia. Some of them had transferred from radio, and specifically Broadcasting House, and seemed a little peeved at being stuck out in the back end of beyond, away from their favourite drinking holes. Broadcasting House was still definitely the 'Holy Grail' and the centre of management, and I and a couple of other 'new boys' were despatched to headquarters to receive training in how the BBC 'worked', its procedures and its systems. I recall that we were given various menial tasks to test our skills; I, for example, like everybody else, was asked to write the weather forecast. I looked at what they had written the day before, and used much the same pattern.

This was then changed by another editor, and sent to the duty editor who promptly changed it all back again to my original draft. It was all rather a nonsense. On another occasion, one of my colleagues, a Romanian Jew, was asked to write a report on the cricket scores. Given his nationality, he had absolutely no idea what cricket was about, or what to do with the myriad of numbers he was presented with, and reported a ridiculous score that could never have been. I saw that the whole exercise was rather pointless, and told my boss that I wasn't going back. His solution was to send me on a week's leave, so that I couldn't cause any more trouble.

Notwithstanding my intolerance for the people at Broadcasting House, I settled in rather well to the routine at Alexandra Palace. One of the television engineers lived close to me in the Chilterns, and we used to share a lift into work. Such was the nature of the BBC at that time that they arranged for our shift patterns to coincide, so that he could always give me a lift. Quite soon I rose up the chain of command and became a senior sub-editor, and began increasingly to work with my colleagues in outside broadcasts. On one afternoon, we had a visit from the head of Soviet television who was on a 'friendship' tour from Moscow. Given that I could speak Russian, it was obvious that we would find ourselves in conversation. One of my jobs on that day was editing one of Khrushchev's speeches from more than two hours to a news item of only two minutes. "But how do you know what to leave in and what to take out?" he asked. I told him it was instinctive. He laughed and said: "I have to write memoranda to my people to tell them what to leave in."

What I imagine would be today called a 'lucky break' came about shortly afterwards, when a vacancy came up for a television outside broadcast producer who spoke foreign languages, and especially French. I was not the most qualified, but neither was I the least qualified, if you see what I mean. I was not ignorant of our colleagues in OB, and had worked with them on a number of occasions when covering a story. Indeed I remember once being invited out with a film crew to report on a woman who had survived a near-fatal accident with a railway engine. She was out driving at three o'clock in the morning, and was approaching a railway bridge, when an engine de-railed and was left dangling above her. It was a miracle she had not been seriously hurt or even killed and so I went to interview her. When I arrived at her house, she was in a frilly pink nightdress and had clearly been on the gin. She agreed to do the interview but only on one condition: I was not to ask who else was in the car with her at the time. When I asked her what was going through her mind at the moment the engine fell off the bridge, she burst into tears and said she had been thinking of her lovely husband. Clearly I surmised it had not been her husband with her in the car, but it made for great television and made the lead story on the London news.

The BBC had visions of expanding into Europe, an idea that was the brainchild of one of the true 'greats' of the BBC, and who was to become my new boss, Peter Dimmock. Peter, like many of us OB producers/directors immediately after the war, was ex-RAF, but unlike me he had been a pilot and a flying instructor. After demob he had joined the Press Association and later the BBC as head of television outside broadcasts. I remember a funny story he used to recount of how he got into journalism. He had originally applied to join Reuters but was unsuccessful. Reuters, however, shared an office with the Press Association, and after telling him there were no jobs at Reuters they literally sent him down to the PA and he was offered a job there, on two weeks notice. He was soon after convinced that the written press and radio were the media of the past, and the future was in television. So he applied for a job at the BBC. The interview panel comprised two former air force officers and a BBC administrator. Peter knew nothing about television, but every time he was asked a question he could not answer, the two ex-air force men would quickly change the subject.

Peter was without doubt the true pioneer of outside broadcasts. He always said that you can brief people as much as you like, but there comes a time when you are on your own, and have to make your own decisions and accept responsibility for your actions. In many ways it was like being in the RAF and a captain of aircraft. You could listen all you liked to the intelligence, navigation and met officers at briefing, but when you were flying 18,000ft over Germany, with the flak flying all around you and the searchlights trying to pick you out in a darkened sky, you had to make your own decisions, and be responsible for the consequences.

As a character, Peter was tough, and did not suffer fools gladly. If he had an opinion he would argue his case vehemently. He was also rather eccentric. On one occasion he demanded that two-way radio was installed in all of the producers' offices, so that he could call down at any time of the day or night and speak to us directly, without having to use the 'traditional' internal phone line. All I did was turn the radio off, which resulted in Peter's hard-working secretary having to hurry along the corridors, telling me to switch it back on as Peter wanted a word.

My first ever live outside broadcast was a boxing match between England and Poland at the Royal Albert Hall. I knew very little about boxing, and very little about outside broadcasting for that matter, and so was more than a little nervous. Harry Carpenter, later to become a legend in BBC sporting circles and already the established 'voice' of boxing, was to be the commentator and told me to have two brandies (not more) before we started. He had only one specific request: in the intervals between each round he would talk about what was happening in the red corner or the blue corner, and I was to cut to the appropriate corner as he spoke. "I don't care much about anything else," he said, "but don't get that wrong." Happily, I didn't, although I did appreciate the irony that the whole fight was being broadcast in black and white, and as such colours were irrelevant.

Harry was old-school and a gentleman. Shortly before the bouts started, I was sitting in the 'scanner' (the word we used to describe our control room) when there was a knock on the door and I was told there was someone who wanted to see me. I didn't want to see anyone but they insisted, and in walked Henry Cooper. Henry wasn't fighting, but had been told by Harry that this was my first event and he had come to wish me good luck. "Don't worry," he told me. "I always used to get a little edgy before a fight, but you'll be fine. Unlike when I fought Ali, everyone is on your side."

As it was the whole event went off without a hitch. The engineers and cameramen knew what they were doing, even if I did not. In those days we only had three cameras to give us wide angles and close up, and effectively I simply followed Harry's commentary to show what he was describing. For some reason, the cameramen who worked in outside broadcasts were called by their Christian names as opposed to 'camera one' or 'camera two', and that was one of the only things that was sometimes difficult for me to remember, but happily on this occasion I seemed to get it right. Half way through the event, I was told that Peter Dimmock was on the phone and wanted to talk to me. I declined. Afterwards, he picked me up on it, and asked me why I had not taken his call. "Well," I said, "You were either calling to tell me I was doing a great job, or a lousy job, but either way I didn't want to know." After the fight had ended, I could sense the relief, and Harry and I went off for dinner in Soho to celebrate.

This was certainly not the only occasion I worked with Harry. When I first met him he was still writing for a newspaper, and no sooner had he finished broadcasting he would have to write his piece for the paper. Harry was very thorough; he always did his homework and was seldom, if ever, caught unaware. A funny thing happened when we were both sent to Moscow. I was in my element as I knew my way around. I knew what restaurants to go to and which to avoid. We visited the Bolshoi to see *Don Quixote*, an evening that Harry described afterwards as one of the best nights of his life. We stayed at a particular hotel near the centre of the city.

Coming down to breakfast one morning, we were approached by two young Armenians who asked us if we were BBC. We were both immediately on our guard, even more so when they asked us if we were sharing or whether we had separate rooms. They explained that they had a couple of girls with them, and wondered whether they could rent our rooms from us while we were working. Needless to say we politely – but firmly – declined.

Because of my language skills, and the fact that I was the only member of the OB team who could speak Russian, I understandably became the 'go to' person whenever there was a relevant story. And at that time in the 1950s/1960s, there were plenty. Peter Dimmock stuck his neck out in working with the Russians, so long as there was reciprocity. If we did something for the Russians, then the Russians had to do something for us. If we covered the annual Red Square Parade, for example, then they would cover the Trooping of the Colour.

A USSR team came to Henley in 1954 for the first time to row at the famous regatta. The coach of their eight was an engaging man with only one leg; he had left the other behind during the fighting at Stalingrad. We got on rather well, even though he had been told not to fraternise with any of the British, and least alone a member of the BBC. He told me that he had heard that English beer was rather good but that he had no money on him to buy any. So I took him to The Angel and bought him a pint. In Russia, he told me, they drink beer with a brandy chaser, so I bought him a brandy to go with it. "Is the BBC poor?" he asked. So I bought him a double. After several pints and more than enough doubles, he said that we must drink *Bruderschaft* and he proposed a toast to "the complete victory of communism throughout the world". I said to him: "Mine is a toast that an old general friend of mine once taught me: 'for the Tsar, for the motherland, and for the faith'. If you will drink to that, then I will drink to yours." At that we linked arms, kissed and drank the toasts, both agreeing that neither statement was likely to come true.

Their visit to Henley, notwithstanding my attempts at comradeship in the pub, was not an especially happy one. The English viewed them with great suspicion and vice versa. A female Soviet doctor who was part of the team was photographed sprinkling some form of powder on her cereal, and the papers were quick to suggest it must have been a performance-enhancing drug. (It did not cross their minds that it might just have been sugar or vitamins.) The Soviets complained about the length of the course, sending the organisers into meltdown. Then they wanted to carry a Soviet flag at the closing ceremony and the good people of the Regatta wouldn't let them.

At Henley you row for your club and not your country, so national flags were not permitted. The chairman of the Regatta asked me for my advice so I told him that the next time the Soviet ringleader (who was obviously KGB) complained, simply enquire which return flight he would like to have arranged and then see what happens. He did as I advised, and they had no further trouble[27]. It was not the most successful trip with regards building closer Anglo-Soviet relations and I did not see my man with the one leg again.

Yuri Gagarin, the Soviet cosmonaut, came to the UK in July 1961, only three months after he had completed his epic encounter with space to become the first man to orbit the earth. While he was here I got to meet him, and we became friendly. He was a quiet, shy and rather modest young man, despite his achievements, and I rather got the feeling that he was somewhat embarrassed to be here. He was undoubtedly proud of being the first man in space, but not so keen to being used as a propaganda tool. He felt like a puppet and of course that was precisely what he was, with the Soviet politicians pulling his strings.

After he died[28] I was invited to Moscow for Gagarin Day (which I believe has since been re-named Cosmonautics Day). The celebration was held in the quite magnificent surroundings of the Kremlin where with much pomp and ceremony they played the national anthem followed by the *Internationale*. Whereas I stood for the anthem, I sat down again for the *Internationale*. A Red Army major at the end of our row of seats shouted at me to stand up. I ignored him, which only made him more agitated, and he continued to shout, at which point I told him to stop. I said to him plainly, in his own language, that whilst I would respect and stand for a national anthem, I would not stand for a political song. This rather sent the man into a frenzy and I was promptly arrested and taken away, though not before a journalist from Reuters, who was sat next to me, whooped with delight that he might have got a scoop.

I was bundled, somewhat roughly, into a waiting black car and driven

27   The USSR, however, did have the last laugh: the Russian eight beat Leander by two and half lengths in the Grand Challenge Cup; a Russian four also beat the RAF in the Stewards Challenge Cup; and the visitors made it a hat-trick of wins by taking the Diamond Challenge Sculls in one of the closest finals ever. A contemporary Pathé news report at the time noted: 'Poor old Britain took a hiding but no-one could say we didn't try!'

28   Gagarin died in 1968 and at the time his death in an air crash was unexplained. In 2013, Aleksey Leonov, a fellow cosmonaut who had been on the official committee to investigate Gagarin's death, revealed the true cause of Gagarin's fatal accident. Another aircraft had flown too close to Gagarin's MiG, and flipped it over with its backwash. The aircraft plunged to the ground at speed, and Gagarin was unable to recover.

to a building some way out of the city. I was taken out of the car and into a small room that had a telephone and a television – neither of which worked. I only had a few copies of **Pravda**, the communist state newspaper, to keep me company. After being kept waiting for about half an hour or so, two Red Army soldiers entered carrying large trays of caviar and smoked salmon and with a bottle of champagne. As incarcerations and abductions go, this one at least seemed to be heading in the right direction, but it was still somehow threatening. Then a senior Red Army officer – a general – came in and we began to talk. He wanted to know why I had refused to stand and whether I was a spy. I made it perfectly clear that I was not a spy, nor had I ever been one, but he was adamant that everyone who worked for the BBC was a spy, and so there was no use me denying it.

After an hour of pleasant conversation, he had to go. I asked what it had all been about. Since I was the supposed expert in Soviet affairs, he found this rather amusing: "Today," he said, "you will learn that Soviet generals are more intelligent than Soviet majors," and with that, he walked out. Happily I was released without further incident or comment. The man from Reuters failed to get his scoop, and was none the worse for his experience.

One story I remember from my many visits overseas for the BBC concerns a piglet that my children christened – for hopefully very obvious reasons – Sir Francis. Near where we lived in Peppard was a farm with a sow that had given birth to a number of piglets. I had been talking to the farmer in the local pub, The Dog, and for reasons that must have been clear at the time agreed that we would adopt the runt. My children spoiled the piglet considerably, training it just like a dog, and it used to sleep on our bed; pigs are actually very clean animals. On returning from Russia on one occasion, I could sense that something was wrong. It took a little while for the story to come out. Sir Francis had been unwell, and the children had given it some of my best brandy (a three-star Martel) through a pipette. Rather than curing the animal, it had actually made matters worse and they were worried that the piglet would die. Happily, he recovered, and we kept him until he became too large to keep in the house and he ultimately went back to the farm.

My work brought me into contact with some of the very greatest journalists and broadcasters of their time, and there was perhaps none greater than the mercurial Richard Dimbleby. Richard had been a journalist all of his working life and even during the war, when he had been an official war correspondent. His voice became familiar on the BBC for his despatches from the front line, either reporting on the progress at El Alamein, or over Berlin with the crew of a Lancaster bomber. Indeed he was reputed to have carried out no fewer than 20 operations with Bomber Command, and held tremendous admiration for the RAF and they for him. It was Richard who Peter turned to for commentary on the coronation, after which he appeared to become the de facto expert on all state occasions. I worked with him whenever there was a big European story, most notably during the first live television broadcast from the Soviet Union in 1961 and on a number of Eurovision projects, of which more later. The secret to Richard's authority was primarily in his preparation. Much like Harry Carpenter, he always did his homework and had plenty of facts and figures at his disposal – all written out on colour-coded cards – in case he needed to fill time – a very necessary skill in television.

In June 1963, we met in Cologne and then in Berlin to cover the visit of President John F Kennedy to what was then West Germany. Richard, being Richard, was staying at the best hotel, and happily the BBC had a rule at that time that allowed us to stay at the same hotel determined by the senior executive. In other words, wherever Richard went, we went too. I recall that two days before Kennedy was due to arrive, Richard announced that he had to fly home, I believe to attend a wedding. One thing I learned very quickly, was that you never argued with Richard. If his mind was made up to do something, then he did it. He promised to be back on time and indeed he was good to his word, but that did not prevent me from having a sleepless night worrying what to do if he were somehow delayed.

To demonstrate his thoroughness, we went out on the eve of Kennedy's arrival and traced the route that the president would take through the city, stopping at every camera position installed by our German engineering colleagues. By each camera he took out his cards and began to make notes of his surroundings – houses, trees, shops – anything to paint a picture in the minds of the listening (and viewing) audience.

In Berlin, Kennedy was due to make his speech on a podium in front of the Schöneberg Rathaus (effectively the city hall) in sight of the infamous Berlin Wall. We obtained permission from the authorities to mount the podium so Richard could see what the president could see and report accordingly. While we were making our preparations, a rather obnoxious British army major with a woman and small child in tow challenged us, and told us we had no right to be there. He then called for an army corporal to forcibly eject us if necessary. At that point Richard asked the major for his regiment and asked him his name. Then very calmly, but with definite menace he said: "I am having dinner with your commanding officer this evening, and we have every right to be here. I will mention your behaviour to him, and in the meantime I suggest that you remove yourself, your woman and your brat from the tower so we can get to work." That was the end to it.

In the event, the broadcast proved yet another triumph. A crowd of some 120,000 Berliners gathered to hear the president make his famous speech of solidarity in which he declared 'Ich bin ein Berliner' to rapturous applause, as the East German border guards looked on from afar in expressionless silence. While Richard could be forthright, he was not without humour. On meeting Yuri Fokin, who was then one of the best-known Russian broadcasters, Fokin said that he was called 'the Richard Dimbleby of Russian television'. Richard replied: "As long as I am not the Fokin of the BBC!"

In the early days of television, we were all experimenting. In the austere times after the Second World War, there was an effective way of sharing skills and resource through what was known as the European Broadcasting Union – popularly known as Eurovision. One of the Eurovision projects that I inherited from my predecessor was a programme called *Carols Around Europe*, a surprisingly popular Christmas show. *Carols Around Europe* was an engineering triumph, successfully being able to cut live coverage from multiple locations (namely churches) in major capitals in the west. I came up with the idea of having a single carol sung by all of the choirs at the same time, and we would cut from one choir to the next. Much to my surprise, it all worked rather well.

(My boss at that time was Aubrey Singer, a wonderful man but inclined to be volatile when pressed. Before we went on air, I said I was going to change my name as the producer. Aubrey was intrigued and asked me what I intended to change my name to. I said: "Moshe Ibinovitch – I think that would look rather fun in the credits." Aubrey made it clear what would happen to me if I chose to be so bold.)

Many of the projects I was involved with were ambitious, not just in their time, but perhaps even today. I covered, for example, the first ever live mountain climb. It was to be undertaken by some French climbers in the Aiguille du Midi, a mountain in the Mont Blanc Massif. We shared the broadcast and the costs with our French colleagues, and so it was agreed that in return a well-respected British climber, Joe Brown (now Joseph Brown CBE – he was sometimes referred to as 'the human fly'), was to be one of the party. It was a tremendous success, and led to other televised climbs, including an ascent of the Old Man of Hoy in the Orkneys.

The French (the same French producer) also wanted to capture an eclipse of the sun which meant filming in Africa at considerable expense. Indeed such was the cost, that the burden was shared between the BBC and our French counterparts. I flew with the French in a small plane to a deserted outpost that had once been a stronghold of the French Foreign Legion. (We needed somewhere with water and electricity.) Its glory days, it is fair to say, were very much behind it, and when I met the president of our host nation I remarked upon it. He said that it was indeed in need of some renovation and promptly provided us with a quote for repairs. It seemed that he had plans to turn the fort into some kind of luxury hotel, and if the BBC could authorise the money to be spent, we could take a share. It was a very attractive offer, but sadly I was obliged to decline.

Sharing production costs was commonplace, but not without its challenges. The Americans, for example, decided to make a programme to mark a particular anniversary of the end of the war in Europe. Creatively, they determined to make the programme from the unique viewpoint of a French village that had suffered more than most. The local mayor was keen; French television was keen; and I was left to ponder the production challenges. On the village square was a small prison where members of the French Resistance had been held and then shot by the Germans. The problem was that my cameras would be shooting into the sun if they wanted the prison to be in view. The American producer asked, in complete seriousness, whether it was possible to move the prison.

I had cause to work with the Americans too on what was to be the first televised footage from space. I was one of the producers responsible at the British end for putting a programme around it, and called upon the services of our resident space expert – and yet another RAF 'type' – Patrick Moore. Between us we felt that the programme needed more weight, and so approached the RAF which had a department in Farnborough that dealt specifically with space. This seemed perfect, and on the first day we were introduced to a squadron leader and all seemed well. He was a shy, diffident character, whose apparent reticence did not last long. On the second day he began suggesting which camera shots we should be using so that on the third day I told him to stick to his job, and I would stick to mine.

I would not want to leave my reader with the impression that my job was especially hard or skilful, or that I was particularly artistic. Much of what we learned, we learned as we went along, by watching and copying others, or by chatting in the canteens and corridors. There was a spirit of sharing. We all recognised that it was the story that mattered. Certainly the producers would come up with the ideas, but the real artists were the technicians – the cameramen, sound engineers, lighting professionals etc. – who had the task of making our ideas work. We might want a camera in a particular place, to get a particular shot, but it was others who worked out whether it was practical.

These men and women took great pride in their work, especially those working in outside broadcasts. On more than one occasion I would hear an exchange from Birmingham or London to the OB team to say that they were getting a bad picture or that the sound wasn't clear, and the engineer would reply "it's leaving us OK," – the implication being that it was the other engineer's fault and not ours.

We had a particularly excellent music department. You could call them, for example, and say that you had a ten-second snow scene in Russia, and could they suggest some appropriate musical accompaniment. They would then send round four or five records with a selection of music, some of which you had never heard of from composers you never knew existed, and it was always perfect. They also had various recordings of known pieces by different conductors. Since all conductors 'conduct' music at their own pace, the precise duration of any given piece could vary. If you needed, therefore, to fill a section for 15 seconds, they could find you the perfect timing of overture to meet your needs. They were exceptionally helpful, as indeed were all of the 'support acts' in the BBC in those early days. I rarely recall ever making a request and being told that it couldn't be done. Someone always found a way somehow, which is why most producers, myself included, treated our colleagues with the utmost respect.

I remember the first three-minute film I made for *Tomorrow's World*, a programme that had been 'invented' by Aubrey Singer, along with *Civilisation* and later that other seminal show *The Ascent of Man* by Jacob Bronowski. Aubrey was a real enthusiast for the sciences, and was instrumental in persuading the BBC to accept that science could be both mainstream and acceptable to a mass audience[29]. The film I was making was in Wales, and I had with me an excellent cameraman. Having spent some time on location with news cameramen, I thought that I knew something about the subject, and started telling the cameraman what to do. This was a mistake. After a little while he asked if he could have a quiet word.

Out of earshot of the rest of the crew, he told me, very politely, that we

29 Aubrey Singer was a straight-talking Yorkshireman who had joined the BBC in 1949. He became controller of BBC 2 in 1974 and later managing director of both BBC Radio and BBC Television. He was described after his death in 2007 as 'the greatest director general the BBC never had'.

could do this one of two ways: if we followed my direction, the entire film would be a cock-up, and I would look like an ass; if we worked on the film together, however, the programme would be a success, and everyone would be telling me what a great director I was. I decided to do things his way and never regretted it. Aubrey said afterwards that I had done rather well with my first film, never knowing quite how close it had been to calamity. It was a lesson well-learned, and I drew many parallels from my time with the RAF. In the RAF you soon came to appreciate that it was the LACs, corporals and sergeants who fixed your engines and kept you from crashing, not the wing commander or adjutant.

Working on short films was a new experience, and I became rather good at it and started to try new things. I always used to cut to the presenter with them standing until one day I saw a presenter walk into shot (a trick they still use to this day). I rather liked it and copied it. One of the bright young things who joined the BBC in 1970 was Patrick Uden. Patrick worked in the science production team as a film director and I always thought of his arrival as marking a turning point, for he was a new breed of professional director whereas I, and many like me, had simply been gifted (and sometimes not so gifted) amateurs. I worked well with Patrick, and on one assignment as we were filming a presenter on the other side of a busy road, a bus drove past and I told them to stop filming. It was Patrick who persuaded me to continue shooting, and that the bus was as much a part of the film as the presenter. He had a completely different way of looking at things.

In those days, the sciences were not recognised in the same way as the arts. Initially, the mistake the BBC made was in staffing science programmes with science people and boffins, rather than people who understood about TV. Slowly the BBC realised that they needed to present science so that it was more accessible to a greater number of people. I worked on the principle that if I understood it, then there was a good chance the ten million viewers might understand it too.

The answer was in dividing the talent so that we had real scientists who did the research, and professional TV people who presented what they had discovered, but in a way that was neither patronising, nor making it sound like a university lecture from a PhD. Steadily we won over both the BBC executive and the general public, and *Tomorrow's World* became one of the most successful TV science programmes of all time. That's not to say that it was all plain sailing; I learned that there was (and probably still is) considerable jealousy within the science community, and not everyone took kindly to what they saw as an early 'dumbing down' of such a serious subject.

The main 'anchor' on *Tomorrow's World* was of course Raymond Baxter whose omnipresence made him somehow synonymous with BBC science and technology programmes in the 1960s and 70s. He had already made a name for himself commentating on the funeral of King George VI (and later Sir Winston Churchill), and reported on the coronation of Queen Elizabeth II. Raymond was yet another former RAF man, but a fighter pilot of some distinction. He was also another who was very thorough in his preparation who became a legend and deservedly so. Mention his name and people would almost genuflect.

Raymond had his faults, and he had his detractors. Because of his experience, and his genuine love of technology (he was an accomplished racing driver and motor enthusiast as well as pilot and probably the only one of us with a technical brain), others could sometimes find him to be a little overbearing. Raymond knew, then he knew that he knew, and that used to irritate. I recall distinctly an occasion when a young researcher suggested certain amendments to his script. Raymond smiled beguilingly, thanked him and said, "F**k off dear boy" with absolute style.

We were very much of the same generation, Raymond and I, and worked together very well for a good number of years not just on *Tomorrow's World,* but also on major events such as the Farnborough Air Show of which he was to become 'the voice'. But Raymond could be stubborn and set in his ways. When an editor once asked him to do a piece about Concorde, with an angle that the new supersonic airliner would be a commercial disaster, he refused to take part. He was so passionate about the aircraft, and the people that built it, that he did not want to be associated with any negative publicity (Raymond flew many times in Concorde, his first when it was still no more than a prototype fuselage. I also accompanied Raymond to the formal launch of the airliner, and have the certificate to prove it). But like anyone in television – as they still find today – no one is bigger than the Corporation, and in the end Raymond had to go. A new editor (Michael Blakstad) described him as "an autocue-reading dinosaur" and Raymond lost his job (Raymond allegedly said that he could never work with someone who came into work on a bicycle). The editor then was all powerful, and to argue with them was not to be advised.

Baxter had joined the RAF aged 18 and was sent for pilot training in Canada and the American Midwest. Returning to the UK with his 'wings' he was posted to 65 Squadron in Scotland to fly Spitfire Vs on shipping reconnaissance sorties over the North Sea. With the landing of Allied forces in North Africa in 1943, Baxter was posted to 93 Squadron to fly the more advanced Spitfire IX in support of the First Army. After a spell as an instructor (a period he later described as "just about the happiest six months of my life"), he returned to operations in September 1944 with 602 Squadron which had only recently been withdrawn from Normandy. From Coltishall in Norfolk he flew against the German 'vengeance' ('V') weapons and was mentioned in a dispatch. While still a serving RAF officer he got his first job in broadcasting as an announcer with the forces broadcasting station in Cairo. He was demobbed in December 1946 with the rank of flight lieutenant.

One editor with whom I worked particularly well and much admired was Alan Dobson. In my mind Alan was the best editor that *Tomorrow's World* ever had, although it took us a little while to understand each other. His idea was simple: if there were to be five items on the programme, then there was to be one that appealed to a child of ten, one for a man of 80 and so on, so that there was something for everyone. Yes we would include what we called a 'hard' science item but that would be complemented by other items that everyone could understand, and that would keep them coming back to watch the following week. It worked. At one time we had audiences of 12 million or more.

The programme went out on a Thursday and was 30 minutes long. Every so often Alan would call me on a Tuesday when he still had a two-and-a-half-minute slot to fill, and it was up to me to come up with a suitable idea or two. I think he came to rely on me to get him out of a hole and somehow I always seemed to come up with something that he liked. I recall one such feature involved a farmer in Poland who had devised a way of growing apple trees such that the branches reached out at right angles. He achieved this by using a clothes peg at the shoot. It was such a wonderfully simple idea and made ideal *Tomorrow's World* viewing. On another occasion we were preparing for an outside broadcast on the Hamble in Hampshire. There was a group of four or five of us standing on a jetty, and somehow I lost my footing and fell in. Of course everyone started to laugh until they realised I couldn't swim. Having been fished out, I told Alan that I would be putting a claim in to the BBC for a new watch and several other items ruined by the water.

Although Raymond was the anchor, and for a time the sole presenter of the show, we later brought in other, younger faces to the team. Names such as Michael Rodd and Judith Hahn will be especially familiar with a particular age of reader and both went on to enjoy successful careers in television. I hope Judith has forgiven me for making her do one of her first ever scenes in a swimming pool full of kids. Another presenter, who shall remain nameless, was rather more of an egotist, who believed that the value of an item was greatly enhanced by him being in the shot. I had to advise him that once you have explained how a device works, the audience next wants to see the device.

Tomorrow's World was responsible for introducing the general public to a good many innovations, from the breathalyser to the pocket calculator. Its success and popularity led to a number of spin-off programmes with which I was involved. I did a programme once about toys for Christmas, a feature that went on to become especially popular and still is. In planning the show I decided it would be a good idea to have children in the item, and so approached a school in Bournemouth to ask them if we could film there. I spoke to the headmistress and asked if they were a multi-racial school, at which she completely misunderstood my motivation for asking and accused me of being racist. Actually it was the other way around: I wanted to make sure that the programme included children from all manner of racial backgrounds so that it was more representative of the country we were living in. As it was, the programme was made and appeared to be a success.

Another programme I made was called *Double Vision* and for the time it was rather a radical concept. I would take individuals with diametrically opposed views and get them to articulate those views to camera. Then I would invite both of them into a studio for further debate. We had a professor and a student; a docker trade unionist and the chairman of the company that owned the shipyard; and my particular favourite, a builder/developer and a retired army colonel whose house was going to be bulldozed to make way for the development.

While filming the programme about the Hull dockers, I became friendly with the union leader, Wally. In the canteen was a sign with 'Jew of the week' written upon it. It was awarded each week to the tightest person in the union. I said that I thought the sign and the sentiment somewhat anti-Semitic and he took it down. Two weeks later, a package arrived at my office. When I opened it, inside was a small wooden shield inscribed with the words 'Jew of the Year 1971'. I kept the shield in my office where it was noticed by one of my seniors, a particularly ambitious young man. He seemed most put out when I explained that it had been awarded to me as a result of a confidential vote by a secret community of fellow Jews, and since he did not know about them it was clear he had not been nominated.

Not every programme I ever made was a success, but my mistakes became fewer and further apart with experience. I also had a few lucky breaks. Once I was obliged to cover a badminton tournament, a game I had never seen before and yet I was expected to film. During one particularly long rally I mistakenly cut to the wrong camera, which showed a close up of the shuttlecock just as it came to rest on the line. It looked intentional, and I was congratulated heartily afterwards for my innovative and prescient thought.

I also worked with a newsreader, a household name both then and today. He was in a most volatile relationship with a woman who operated the autocue. It was well known that if they had had a row, she would express her displeasure at him by slowing or accelerating the autocue, much to our amusement.

On another occasion I once received a memorandum from Sir Hugh Greene, the director general of the BBC and brother of the novelist, Graham Greene. The memo simply read: 'I watched your film last night and could see what you were trying to do. I think you failed. Good luck in the future.'

Indeed this was not the only occasion that I had cause to come across my boss. I was still the 'go to' man when it came to liaising with our Soviet television colleagues and my services were called upon to help Sir Hugh on a visit to Moscow to meet his opposite number. He had asked for an interpreter, and although the Soviets said that they had their own, somebody high up thought better of it and decided to send me along to keep an eye on things. A visa was arranged for me in some haste, so that I met Sir Hugh and his wife at the airport in Moscow without him knowing I would be there. (Hopefully it was a pleasant surprise.)

On his visit to the Soviet television studios, he was asked whether he would address the senior executives on the floor. At this point Sir Hugh turned to me and said that since I was the expert, what should he say? I said that he should tell the executives that even as director general, you cannot be aware of every programme that is being made, and that sometimes you can switch on your television and watch something and think 'Gosh there's going to be trouble in the morning'. This seemed to appease him and so we went to lunch where I proceeded to drink rather more than my fill. This would have been fine had not the DG then insisted that I made a speech to the assembled throng. I attempted to politely decline but it was made very clear that I didn't have a choice and so rose somewhat unsteadily to my feet and started to speak in Russian, pausing to translate as I went along.

I of course said that we were delighted and honoured to be there, and that I hoped very much that the collaboration agreement that had been signed between the head of the BBC and the head of Soviet television would turn into action, and that the lofty sentiments signed by such eminent men would filter down to unimportant producers such as myself so that we could all benefit. I sat down to rapturous applause led, I am pleased to say, by our own director general.

(One further story of Sir Hugh's visit to Moscow involved the hotel where he and his wife were staying. Despite being one of the most expensive and luxurious in Russia, Sir Hugh complained to me that they could never get the breakfast that they wanted. I came in that evening and spoke to the waiter about it, and he assured me all would be well. The following day I asked whether the order had been fulfilled and it had not. When I went in to complain again, the waiter was not the same man I had spoken to the day before, and he had left no instructions to his successor. Such was the way in Russia in those times.)

My visits to Moscow were fairly frequent while in the BBC's employ. One occasion I remember in particular involved a group of Cubans. I had been invited to the National Hotel, the only really decent hotel in Moscow, to a dinner as a guest of the Soviet foreign minister, a signal honour. I think I was popular with them because I tried as far as possible to work with them, and not against them. It was late, and our civilised dinner was suddenly interrupted by a group of half a dozen or so Cubans, all dressed in khaki battledress and wearing their distinctive square caps – mirror images of their leader and hero Fidel Castro.

The Cubans were an especially noisy bunch who made their presence felt. Other diners began to rise in approval and shout out in chorus 'Cuba si. Yankee no!' The noise became deafening and the foreign minister asked them to join our table, as the chanting continued. Being British, and disinclined to badmouth our allies, I kept quiet but my silence drew the Cubans' attention. One of them turned to me and the conversation went something like:

"You no like Cuba?"
"Yes I like Cuba a lot."
"Then why don't you join in?"
"Because I am British and am not going to chant 'Yankee no'."

At that point we realised upon a compromise and started to shout out "Cuba si. Britain si! Cuba si. Britain si!" – banging the table in time as we did so. My new-found Cuban friends began to chant with us, and before I knew it, all of the hotel diners were shouting out in turn. The next day the whole of Moscow was talking about it and I happened to come across our

British ambassador who was delighted with the turn of events. He said I had achieved more for Anglo-Cuban diplomacy in five minutes than the British diplomatic service had achieved in five years.

I was also in Moscow for the historic visit of Sir Harold Wilson, the British prime minister, to meet the Russian premier. Following negotiations *Panorama* had secured a live event to be broadcast to the world and I was to be the producer. I flew out with a small team a few days in advance to ensure that the 'Moscow end' was set up and that there were no problems. Wilson arrived and went to the embassy where he met with a senior Soviet delegation for talks behind closed doors. I was on the outside looking in, waiting for the talks to end so that we could drive the prime minister to the studio for a live interview. But Wilson would not be hurried, and as I looked at my watch, I became increasingly concerned that we would run out of time. I had visions of what Paul Fox, the controller of BBC One[30] was going to do to me on my return if I came back with nothing. Then, just when I thought we really would miss our opportunity, the doors opened, and Wilson and his entourage, the Russians included, came sweeping down the stairs. The Soviets at last departed, and I was standing in a moment of history, waiting for the prime minister to say something befitting of the occasion. Instead, all I heard was one of his party splutter: "One of those Russians has stolen my gin!" Despite the farce, Wilson did eventually make the studio on time and the interview was a great success. It was, I believe, the first time that a British prime minister had been televised live from Moscow.

I spent quite a time at the British embassy whenever I was in Moscow on business, and always seemed to get on delightfully well with the ambassador and his staff. I think they liked me because I understood the Russians as well, and probably even better, than they did, and as such rather than being a nuisance I was more often than not a great help. There was one incident I particularly recall when I was present for the Queen's birthday. I had no responsibilities as such, but was simply there as a guest. The barometer of Anglo-Soviet relations could be measured by the seniority of the Soviet officials who attended: First secretary, and you knew things were at their best; fifth or sixth, and relations were at something of a nadir. I was happily chatting away to a Soviet guest and after I had finished one of the senior secretaries of the British embassy asked me:

"What is your nationality? I am puzzled."
"English," I replied.
"My dear boy," he continued, "British you might be. English never."

---

30   From 1967 – 1983. Later Sir Paul Fox CBE.

He was astute but tactless, and on that basis probably went on to enjoy a successful career in the diplomatic service. In fairness, it wasn't quite meant as intended, and he did very soon afterward apologise.

The US embassy was guarded by US Marines. Being marines they always seemed to have a racket going on and that included a select club into which no foreigners were allowed admittance other than a handful of Scandinavian au pairs. The American club sold English and American cigarettes that could not be bought anywhere else in Moscow, and as a smoker at that time I asked if I could buy some. Unfortunately all they had were some Lucky Strikes, and they were not to my taste. A man standing nearby overheard my conversation and asked if I'd like some English cigarettes. I nodded eagerly at which point the man disappeared, only to return shortly afterwards with a carton of 200 Senior Service. I asked him how much I owed, and he said nothing. He was, he explained, the ambassador's butler. I thanked him nonetheless.

Three or four days later, I was invited to lunch with the ambassador and after our meal we adjourned to the library for a brandy. We passed a very pleasant hour in each other's company before it was time to go. Before I left he asked me whether there was anything else I wanted. I said that I wouldn't mind some English cigarettes, and he rang the bell for the butler. The butler came in and the ambassador asked whether he had some cigarettes to spare. "I am afraid not," the butler said. "If we gave cigarettes to every itinerant BBC man in Moscow we would very quickly run out and have none for ourselves." I was somewhat surprised but did not make a fuss until afterwards when the butler walked me to my car. "I've got something for you," he said, and thrust a bag into my hands containing two more cartons of Senior Service. 'But I thought you didn't have any to spare," I said. "What was all that palaver about in the library." "Ah well you see sir, when it comes to matters of diplomacy, Anglo-Soviet relations and foreign affairs, that's his Excellency the Ambassador's department; if it's cigarettes, toothpaste or soap, then you come to me."

Cigarettes, toothpaste and soap were indeed luxury items in Russia and commanded a high price. Fresh produce – cucumbers, tomatoes, radishes and so forth – were in plentiful supply, but such was the paranoia of the British and Americans in Moscow that they preferred to only use produce that had come from home. A teacher that I knew (she taught in a US school for children of American diplomats and their staff) had a larder that was always well stocked with food, US food, but she never had any fresh vegetables in the house because she had been warned that they might be poisoned. I went with her to the local market and bought her anything she wanted, which included the first cucumber she had seen for more than six months.

In 1980, shortly before I retired, I was in Moscow to help cover the Olympic Games, a controversial affair since it did not include athletes from the United States. Their country had opted to boycott the games in protest at the Soviet invasion of Afghanistan (the irony not being lost on today's generation). We were once again part of the Eurovision network, reaching 31 countries including the UK, and I was there principally to act as a 'bridge' between the Russian broadcasters and our own.

Every morning we would be driven by the Soviets to the main stadium, and on every occasion, we were taken to a different gate. It all seemed very petty at the time and most frustrating for my Eurovision colleagues, but they just had to accept it and move on. There may have been legitimate security reasons for changing the schedules, though it is more likely to have been a show of strength, in case we doubted who was in charge.

Security was, in fact, rather tight. Olympic Games had been targeted before both by terrorists and by every protest movement imaginable, and the Soviets were determined that no such demonstrations or attacks would mar their perfect showpiece event. On arrival at the stadium, we would walk through a scanner, a process familiar to anybody who has been through an airport. One of our German colleagues, however, had a pacemaker or some other medical device that set the machine off every time, and every time he was then searched. Clearly he found this all somewhat humiliating, and asked if I could intervene. I managed with some negotiation for the Soviet security people to allow him through, and asked whether he might be given a letter to exempt him from being searched in the future. "You know a lot about Russia," the officer said to me, "But do you really think a Russian colonel is going to give a written instruction for a foreign journalist not to be searched? You are mad." My German friend did not get his letter but did not get searched again.

The Moscow games were not the first Olympics that I covered. Sixteen years earlier, in the summer of 1964, I had worked on the Tokyo games with Cliff Michelmore. Cliff was a delight to work with and a consummate professional. He understood that television was all about working as a team, and that you were only as good as your weakest link. He also had a tremendous sense of humour, and this often carried us through some trying experiences.

The Tokyo games were certainly 'trying'. They were the first to be 'telecast' internationally without the need for tapes to be flown all over the globe as they had been four years earlier. The games were telecast to the United States using the first geostationary communications satellite, and from there to Europe. In preparation, Aubrey Singer sent me to Europe some weeks in advance to explore the best location, weather-wise, to receive our transmission. This involved cruising around Europe being treated as a lord until I determined that the airport at Hamburg was the perfect site. German television was especially excited and keen to help, and provided me with my own interpreter, unaware that I spoke their language fluently. On my first evening, we went for a drink, and she seemed rather distant and concerned. Naturally I asked her what was wrong and she said that she knew that I spoke German, but if the others found out then she would lose her job. From then on I played dumb and nobody was any the wiser. (Her father, I later learned, had been a high-ranking Nazi official, and when she found out she walked out of their house and never saw him again. Later still I believe she became a surgeon of some renown.)

My time at the BBC came to an end a year short of what would have been my 60th birthday on January 20, 1983. I did not, at that stage, have any idea what I wanted to do but had been approached by a public relations company, Carl Byoir, to become one of the first ever account executives to focus solely on attaining television coverage for their clients. It all sounded rather interesting but on reflection I should have known that it was doomed to fail. The PR company did not understand television or how it worked, and believed that once they engaged with the television producers, they would be able to pitch stories on their terms. I sat in a good many meetings and made a number of introductions, but the company never seemed to grasp the basic fact that they needed the television companies much more than the television companies needed them. After 18 months of achieving very little, I was sacked.

A chance conversation with a lady in a pub led me into something that would end up being my third career, although one with echoes of my past life in the prisoner-of-war camps. She worked for the police as an interpreter and knew that I spoke several languages. The police, she said, and the various enforcement agencies then under the control of the Home Office, were often in need of foreign language experts and she gave me a number to call. I did exactly that, and was sent a form to fill in and before I knew it I was officially engaged.

The job was an excellent one, and matched both my talents (such as they were) and my interest. I would use my Polish, Russian and German to assist the police and immigration officials whenever it was needed. Police stations and national airports, notably Gatwick and Heathrow, became my second homes, as did the courts. I was freelance, and the hours were never nine to five, but again that was not an issue. I was paid by the hour, so I would go wherever I was sent, including on occasion to Belfast.

In my role as an official translator I had to be non-partisan, non-judgmental and neutral. There were occasions when certain officials might try and exert pressure on me to give them an opinion as to somebody's guilt or otherwise, or ask me to guess at whether they were telling the truth, but I would always answer truthfully that I was there to interpret, and not to give an opinion or assist with an arrest. There was a case of a Russian who arrived in the UK and was being held at immigration, pretending to be a Pole. For a period of time it was easy to cross over from Russia into Poland and acquire yourself a Polish passport and a new identity, and then head for the UK. It became clear immediately that this man pretending to be Polish was in fact Russian, but I did not offer an opinion as to his nationality, I simply translated what he said. I did ask him how he could be Polish and not speak Polish, to which he replied that he knew many Poles who could not speak the Polish language, I suppose as some British people today cannot speak English. I do not know what became of him or whether his 'secret' was finally exposed.

Occasionally at Heathrow, immigration officers would stop a Romany family and take the father to one side to have a quiet conversation. It was all very polite and civilised; no offence had been committed, and I would be called upon to translate. On one such occasion I explained to the Romany father the nature and purpose of the interview, to which he refused to answer any questions unless and until his solicitor was present, at which point he handed over the calling card of a well-known London solicitor who would represent his case.

The most responsible part of my job was when called upon to go to court, including the Crown Court. Then you realised that the future of the individual you were representing could depend on the accuracy of your translation. It meant dealing with all sorts of people in all sorts of scenarios, and much like my career in television, I found I got better at it as I went along.

I only stopped translating on my 90th birthday, principally because I had to give up my car and so could no longer travel about with such ease. It coincided with a move by the Home Office to outsource translations to a private company, rather than using freelancers, and so the writing was already on the wall. And thus I retired again for what would be the final time.

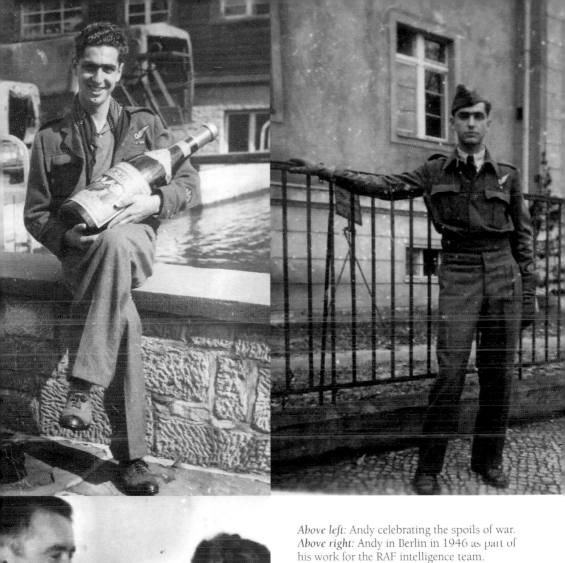

Above left: Andy celebrating the spoils of war.
Above right: Andy in Berlin in 1946 as part of his work for the RAF intelligence team.
Left: Russians at Luckenwalde, the camp where Andy was the interpreter.

Top left: Andy poses in front of a Dakota on his way home after the war.
Below left: Andy on duty in Berlin.
Below right: Flight Sergeant Bill Lyall.
Opposite top: Outside the headquarters of the RAF Disarmament Flight set up to assess German weaponry and equipment.
Opposite bottom: Members of the RAF Intelligence team. Andy was part of a small team who helped to track down one of the murderers of 'the fifty'.

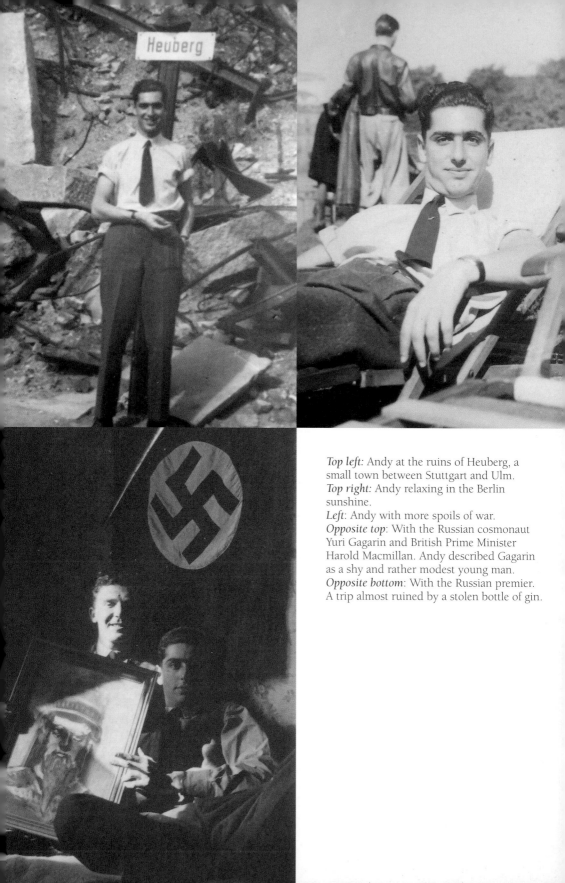

Top left: Andy at the ruins of Heuberg, a small town between Stuttgart and Ulm.
Top right: Andy relaxing in the Berlin sunshine.
Left: Andy with more spoils of war.
Opposite top: With the Russian cosmonaut Yuri Gagarin and British Prime Minister Harold Macmillan. Andy described Gagarin as a shy and rather modest young man.
Opposite bottom: With the Russian premier. A trip almost ruined by a stolen bottle of gin.

Top: Andy meeting the Duchess of Cornwall alongside Charles Clarke.
Left: With Prince Charles a[t] *Tomorrow's World* studios.
Opposite top: Andy receivi[ng] the Bomber Command cla[sp] from Prime Minister David Cameron.
Opposite bottom: Andy at Zagan for the 70th Anniversary of the Great Escape in 2014.

Above: Andy at the site where h[...]
Halifax came down.
Left: Andy at Zagan with Alfie
Fripp and other veterans.
Below left: The family at Andy'[...]
90th birthday party.

LOTNIKOM ALIANCKIM
JENCOM STALAGU LUFT III
UCZESTNIKOM
WIELKIEJ UCIECZKI

ZAGAN 2004

25.03
1944

CHAPTER SEVEN

RETURN TO ZAGAN

I have never much been one for reunions and had no particular desire to return to Zagan or reminisce with fellow POWs until I saw an advertisement in a national newspaper that pricked my conscience. It was an appeal by Sydney Dowse, one of the greatest of the great escapers, to former prisoners of war at Zagan to attend a memorial service at St Clement Danes to commemorate the 50th anniversary of the Great Escape. Sydney not only organised but also financed the whole affair, including a champagne reception at the RAF Club. It was a most successful event that I was delighted to attend.

Since then I was determined to return to Zagan, and have now been back on a number of occasions, often in the company of Air Commodore Charles Clarke, the chairman of the ex-POW Association who had himself been shot down in February 1944 while attacking Schweinfurt. There has been much interest in the Great Escape, especially recently with the 70th anniversary commemorations, and a number of exciting projects to ensure that the memory of the event and the 50 men who were murdered are never forgotten.

Sydney Dowse joined the RAFVR is 1937, and on the outbreak of war flew with Coastal Command on anti-submarine patrols. At the end of 1940 he volunteered to join a Photographic Reconnaissance Unit (PRU) flying Spitfires at very high altitudes. In September 1941, whilst on a sortie to photograph the German warships *Scharnhorst* and *Gneisenau* he was shot down, wounded and captured. Dowse escaped from the hospital in which he was being treated but was caught and sent to Stalag IXC but got away again. Recaptured once more he was imprisoned in Oflag VIB, helping to build four tunnels, before being moved again to Stalag Luft III. He was the 21st man to exit the Great Escape tunnel, and after two weeks on the run he was finally recaptured, along with his escape partner 'Danny' Krol. Krol was executed; Dowse sent to Sachsenhausen concentration camp. Remarkably, he escaped from Sachsenhausen, was recaptured and put in chains for five months in solitary. Moved to Dachau and then the Tyrol, he was finally liberated by Allied forces in May 1945. He was awarded the Military Cross (MC) for his activities as a prisoner.

The main project I was involved with was to build a replica of Hut 104, the hut from which the Great Escape took place. The brainchild of military historian Dr Howard Tuck along with a serving officer, Flight Lieutenant Tim Barlow, I was in Zagan, with Charles, when it was first discussed in 2006. The idea was to build the replica on the site of the original hut, but it soon became clear that this was neither practical nor desirable, and a better site was found nearer to the camp museum. A substantial sum of money was raised in donations (in no small part through the ex-POW Association) and the team recruited an experienced engineer, Lieutenant Colonel Phil Westwood RE to ensure that the hut was constructed to the precise technical specification of the original.

The team was broadened to include a group of enthusiastic amateur builders from the RAF, RE and RN; I was also given the honour of driving in a nail in a symbolic act of solidarity with the build team. The volunteers were split into two groups – appropriately called Dick and Harry – working in shifts, for a period of two weeks until the hut was completed. A ceremony was held on August 16, 2008, with Charles and I as guests of honour, to celebrate the official opening, and I have to admit that the occasion brought back memories, some of them good, some of them bad, about the war years and those that we left behind.

The fall of the Iron Curtain has made things much easier for parties to visit Zagan, and the Polish military always pull out all of the stops for our reunions. It has also had an impact on one of the local schools. Schools in communist Poland had numbers rather than names and in recent times they have been allowed to choose new identities for themselves. Rather touchingly, the local school voted to call itself the School of Allied Aircrew in memory of the thousands incarcerated in Stalag Luft III. Charles and I again were pleased to be at the formal opening, and the school is now part of our route each year when we commemorate the Long March.

Indeed the Long March is an event that has received considerable interest in recent times after almost 70 years of being forgotten, except by those of us who were there. One of the driving forces behind a series of commemorations and re-enactments is Neil Galloway MBE, a good friend to the ex POW Association and a good friend to me. Neil's story is an interesting one in itself. He was until recently serving in the RAF as a tactical communications engineer. After 25 years he resigned to become a priest (he is a Catholic archdeacon) but maintains his links with the RAF and one day soon hopes to rejoin the service as a full-time chaplain.

Neil is also closely involved with the prison service, and in particular working with those prisoners who are ex-servicemen as they prepare to re-integrate into society towards the end of their sentences. He does this through an organisation called Veterans in Custody Support (VICS), and involved Charles and I in speaking to the prisoners and sharing our experiences of the war and our captivity. He describes it as 'ex-prisoners of war meeting ex-servicemen in prison'.

Neil was involved with Howard Tuck in the Hut 104 project, and in the 65th anniversary of the Great Escape. He also took the service for the funeral of Alfie Fripp. But perhaps his most noteworthy achievement was in arranging a re-enactment of the Long March for a party of ex-servicemen at HMP Kirklevington Grange in North Yorkshire. For obvious reasons he could not take them to Germany, so replicated the march as accurately as he could in the Yorkshire countryside, with the prisoners accompanied by prison officers who were also ex-servicemen and current serving RAF officers. It was a tremendous accomplishment and raised money for a number of good causes including Combat Stress.

In 1993 I was contacted by the 466 Squadron Association which was raising funds to have a memorial erected in memory of the Australian and British aircrew who flew with both 166 and 426 Squadrons. I was subsequently invited to an unveiling of a black stone that they had shipped in from Australia, and was honoured to lay one of the first wreaths. During the ceremony, a RAF padre gave the usual benediction that made reference to Christian courage. I could not help myself from asking him what the difference was between Christian or Jewish courage, and why it had to be specified so. His only answer was that it was part of the sermon, and although it might indeed need re-writing, it was unlikely to change in the immediate future.

Having been re-acquainted with the squadron I journeyed to Luckenwalde with Bruce Loane, a fellow 466 Squadron contemporary and Luckenwalde Kriegie who had been shot down in December 1943. The camp was at that time still a Russian army base, and I struck up a conversation with the Russian orderly officer to see if he would let us in. We arranged to go back the following day, and we were indeed given a three-hour guided tour of the camp by the Russian commanding officer and his staff who were most charming. The camp had of course changed a great deal since our enforced 'stay', but there was plenty that we still recognised, including the German quarters and the appel ground.

During the same visit we also arranged to meet Heinz Rokker, the pilot who had been responsible for ending Bruce's war. Rokker had been one of the Luftwaffe's very best nightfighters, credited with shooting down some 63 aircraft, including Halifax HX273 in which Bruce had been flying and in which his skipper, Pat Edwards, had been killed. I cannot speak for Bruce, but it was a strange sensation to be sitting and talking to someone who was once your sworn enemy. We exchanged stories and experiences well into the night.

At Elvington, a former 4 Group base and now home to the Yorkshire Air Museum, I had a chance to see its Halifax up close, one of the only such aircraft that exists anywhere in the world. Actually, to be fair, it is not 'one' Halifax but rather made up of the pieces of several aircraft, the heart of which is the mid-fuselage section that had served as a henhouse on the Isle of Lewis. Notwithstanding its provenance, it is a remarkable aircraft, and being so close after so long I had forgotten what monsters they were. I wanted to clamber inside, but was refused permission on grounds of health and safety. If only the health and safety police had been around 70 years earlier, I might never have been shot down.

I have never had any qualms about the bombing war, or my own role as an air bomber. Given that the Nazis had murdered my father and my whole family with the exception of my mother, my view was that if I could have done anything to shorten the war by even five minutes, I would have done it. It helped that the people we killed were anonymous; we dropped our bombs from 18,000ft and never saw the consequences of our actions. My vision of war was primarily one of huge explosions and equally large fires. Had I seen burned children perhaps I may have had some doubts, but wars cannot be fought by Queensberry Rules and I was determined to be on the winning side.

Of course it was a disgrace that after the war our own commander-in-chief, Arthur Harris, was denied the accolades that must surely have been rightfully his. So too did we suffer as a result of the politicians' needs to re-write history, and distance themselves from the bomber boys. We were convenient scapegoats; pariahs. For 70 years we were denied a campaign clasp; we were also denied our memorial, and our right to be treated on equal terms with our contemporaries in the army, navy, and even some parts of the RAF. While the media focused on the exploits of 'The Few', the contribution of Bomber Command to eventual victory was swept under the carpet and all but forgotten.

What brought about this change of heart I do not know, but when Charles was organising a party of veterans in March 2013 to receive their clasp from the prime minister, David Cameron, I was one of the lucky few to be invited. A small group of us met at the RAF Club and were coached to Number Ten along with the chief of air staff. We were shown into a large room that had chairs set out in rows for the aircrew, their friends and families. The prime minister made a short but appropriate speech in which he quoted from Winston Churchill, and then pinned the clasp onto my Aircrew Europe Star. Alongside my bejewelled golden caterpillar, given to me for surviving a parachute jump by the equipment manufacturers Irvin, it is one of my proudest possessions.

This was not the first time I had met Mr Cameron. I had been introduced to him the year before at the unveiling of the Bomber Command Memorial in Green Park. When I heard that they were planning to build a memorial I was rather concerned as to what it might be. Any reservations that I did have, however, were swept away when I saw it, a magnificent sculpture of a group of aircrew, looking to the skies for their comrades who have failed to return. The memorial is neither victorious, nor gloating. It is respectful, and articulates precisely what all of us felt: that the most important part of any raid was to make it home in one piece.

The opening service was a wonderful occasion, but my view of Her Majesty the Queen was somewhat obscured by the bush hats of a group of former RAAF aircrew. But just as I was about to say something, one of them turned around, looked at me and said: "Bloody hell it's Andy!" I was thus reunited with some of my former squadron pals from 466. At a reception after the unveiling, the prime minister said that I must have felt very proud. I told him that I was, but that it was a great pity that not a single mother was alive to share in that day, to see the nation honour the sons that they had lost. He understood. I am pleased to have the clasp, and delighted with the memorial, but my pleasure has been diminished by the length of time that these honours have taken.

There is one more thing that I mentioned to the prime minister: I told him that the government still owed me, and hundreds like me, money. When we came back from the war, we are all given our back pay, but that pay was short. This resulted from a claim by the Germans that in the officers' camp at Stalag Luft III we dined handsomely on fresh meat, fruit and eggs and always had fresh milk to drink. The British government paid the German government accordingly. When it transpired we had not been treated to such fine foods, the Air Ministry demanded the money back from the German authorities with the intention of its re-distribution to former POWs. The ministry, however, seemed to have lost the nominal roll, and so could not reimburse us. Although we created our own roll, we were told that it could not be seen as 'official'. And so the money still resides with the ministry. It is not the monetary value that is important – although even a shilling a day for a year with accrued interest over 70 years will make a welcome bonus – it is the principle. These men suffered for their country, and ever since their return they have had to fight to achieve everything that should have been given to them without qualm or question.

At a book signing event two years ago I was delighted to meet Derek Camp, the son of our flight engineer Jack. Derek had made considerable efforts to research his father's RAF career and had also located the crash site of our Halifax, LV956, in France. A local museum recovered some artefacts from the crash, and was delighted to hear that I was still alive. I now have in my possession a small piece of that aircraft, and have it mounted for display.

Somewhat by chance I was invited to contribute to a cookbook being published by the Help for Heroes charity. The premise of the book was simple: you nominated your hero and put forward your favourite recipe. My hero was and is Major Mordechai Anielewicz, the commander of the Jewish Fighting Organisation (ZOB) and leader of the ill-fated Warsaw uprising. My recipe was for chicken noodle soup. Since the book was published I have not been criticised for my choice of hero, but several Jewish women seem unhappy with the way I cook my soup.

In September 2014 I returned to Berlin, the city of my birth. I walked along the Innsbrucker Straße, past the point where I used to torment the SA officer and his dog. I visited my old school, the Werner Siemens Gymnasium, renamed in 1956 after a Silesian businessman, Georg von Giesche. The school well remembers its heritage. Above one of the doors is a photomontage of former pupils and a brief history that confirms that the school was closed by the Nazis in 1935. The official reason was given as 'lack of pupils'. It did not help, perhaps, that in my street alone some 125 Jewish pupils had been arrested. I also went to the memorial for the Berlin Jews who were deported, and rested awhile among the rectangular blocks, and remembered.

Just before Christmas I also returned to France with the son of my flight engineer, Derek Camp. We visited the place where my Halifax came down and where it is planned to erect a memorial in 2015 to the crew and especially those who did not make it home. I was also able to visit their graves.

So as I sit now, more than 70 years after the war and in my 93rd year, and reflect on the incidents and personalities who shaped my life, I think primarily about how lucky I have been, to be one of the survivors. I think in particular about my time in the RAF, how it has left a lasting impression and made me what I am today. Although I was only in the Royal Air Force for a comparatively short space of time, in that time I learned that obstacles in life are there to be surmounted, not ignored. However difficult they might seem at first, no obstacle is ever too great. In the armed forces you wear a uniform, but that does not mean that you have to blindly do as you are told, at least not in the junior service. You learn to respect the man, rather than the rank, and to obey those orders that you agree with. These are all lessons that I took with me into civilian life, often to the dismay of my superiors, but nearly always to the satisfaction of my equals.

I regret, perhaps, that I never mastered *The Wind in the Willows* and probably never shall. I am grateful for *The Charge of the Light Brigade* for teaching me the joys of onomatopoeia (even though I still can't spell it). And I still find pleasure and understanding in *Julius Caesar*. These three texts that I studied on my arrival into the UK were the first steps in making me less of an alien.

There is a line in *Julius Caesar* that goes: '...the evil that men do lives after them; the good is oft interred with their bones...'

I would like people to think the opposite of me: that any good that I might have done will live on, and any evil is buried and forgotten.

———————

Only a few short few weeks after the manuscript of *An Alien Sky* was finished, Andy Wiseman died unexpectedly after a very short illness. It was two days after his 92nd birthday. Andy is buried next to his wife Jean, to whom this book is dedicated, at the Parkside Cemetery in Gerrards Cross, Buckinghamshire. The last lines of this book, how Andy wished to be remembered, were read out as part of the celebration of Andy's life.

THE CREW

The pilot – Flight Sergeant Barry Casey – killed in action

Barry William Casey was born on April 11, 1920 to Marie and Denis Casey, and raised a Roman Catholic in the town of Newcastle, New South Wales. Attending the local Commercial College, Barry was a keen all-round sportsman, with a particular aptitude for football, tennis, cricket and hockey, and matched his sporting prowess with a keen brain. He sat for the Intermediate Public Examination in November 1936 achieving passes in maths (I and II), English, business principles and geography – qualifications that would stand him in good stead for what was to follow. He studied further at the Sydney Tech Ultimo, taking courses in motors and construction, before embarking on a career as a motor mechanic and a salesman.

With the outbreak of war, and the more immediate threat to his homeland from the Japanese in the Pacific that presaged Pearl Harbor, Barry joined a local militia as a sapper, before enrolling in the reserve of the Royal Australian Air Force on July 9, 1941, having applied for aircrew training the month before. Four months later he was formally enlisted into the RAAF at No 2 Recruiting Centre in Woolloomooloo, Sydney and after a medical that passed him fit for pilot training, posted to 2 Initial Training School to learn the basics of service life.

Barry's flying training started on Tiger Moths at 8 Elementary Flying Training School (8 EFTS) at Narrandera in New South Wales in April 1942 (Course 24), progressing to the more advanced 1 Service Flying Training School (1 SFTS) at Point Cook in June 1942 where he was awarded his wings in October. At this time he had advanced from single-engine bi-planes to the more sophisticated twin-engined monoplane (the Airspeed Oxford) in preparation for flying multi-engined aircraft on operations.

With the first part of his flying training completed, Barry was posted from 1 SFTS to No 2 Embarkation Depot (2 ED) at RAAF Bradfield Park, and thence onwards to No 1 Embarkation Depot (1 ED) in Ascot Vale, where he set sail from Melbourne on January 15, 1943 for the long voyage to the UK via New York. Arriving on March 26, 1943, Barry was posted to an advanced flying unit (20 [P] AFU) to familiarise himself with the hazards of flying in blacked-out skies and wartime conditions. While at AFU he was briefly attached to 1515 BAT Flight to learn the intricacies of blind approach, before being posted to 21 OTU to be crewed up.

Throughout his training his character was consistently rated as 'very good' and his proficiency 'satisfactory', from his initial rank as an aircrafthand (ACH) through to his promotion to flight sergeant. In addition to his operations with 466 Squadron, Barry is also reported to have flown a single trip from Elvington with Flight Sergeant J E Richards. Richards was shot down and killed in a raid over Frankfurt. Barry is buried at a cemetery in Poix-de-la-Somme.

The navigator – Flight Sergeant 'Bob' Wallace – evaded

John Robert 'Bob' Wallace was older than many of his contemporaries when he volunteered to join the RAAF, but still only 25 when he formally enlisted and was posted to 2 ITS (29 Aircrew Course Observers) for his initial training on June 20, 1942. Bob had applied for aircrew training at the end of 1941, and accepted as fit for training as air observer or air gunner. He grew impatient while he waited his turn, so much so that he wrote to the authorities asking to be released for service in another unit.

Born on April 6, 1917 in Sydney, he was indeed as intelligent as Andy surmised, having attained his Intermediate in 1930 with passes in English, maths, geometry, algebra, physics and chemistry. Like Barry, he was keen on his sport, and especially rugby league and swimming. Upon leaving school he attended the Sydney Technical College to study engineering, and was originally apprenticed to the New South Wales Government Railway (NSWGR) with skills in fitting and turning. He was later a partner in a local firm, the Goulburn Engineering Company.

When called for training the wheels moved quickly, but whereas Barry was trained in Australia, Bob was sent overseas to Canada, embarking from Brisbane at the beginning of October 1942. He was posted firstly to 3 Navigation School (3 N) and then 2 Air Observers School (2 AOS), both in Edmonton, attached to the Royal Canadian Air Force (RCAF). Awarded his navigator's brevet on March 5, 1943 at the end of his course, he journeyed to the UK via Halifax in Nova Scotia, arriving on April 4. He arrived at 21 OTU via RAF West Freugh in Wigtownshire, an AFU for observers. At both OTU and 1652 HCU, Bob received favourable reports from his instructors, and was noted as being suitable for a commission in due course.

On the night their aircraft was shot down, Bob was the first to bale out, and witnessed the aircraft crash and explode. In a letter to Ken Lyall, a relative of the mid-upper gunner, Bob wrote: 'The drill on landing was to get as far enough as possible from the crash site by dawn and then hide up for the next day and then move on further south, towards Switzerland or Spain. On starting out at dusk the next night I walked by accident into a farm yard and was held up by the farmer, who fortunately, was a member of the French Resistance who arranged for me to join one of their groups, and who over a period of weeks forwarded me further south to Paris.'

Bob crossed the Spanish border on the afternoon of May 28 in the company of several American airmen and two members of the RAF. They were taken into custody the next day at the village of Les and after an overnight stay in a local hotel, were escorted to Viella. From Viella they went by truck to Sort, where Bob was temporarily separated from the group and housed with a party of refugees, the authorities being under the misapprehension that Bob was Austrian. On June 3, Bob left Sort by bus for Lérida, and stayed in another hotel for ten days having initially being taken to the local gaol pending the arrival of the British consul. From Lérida, Bob journeyed to Alhama in the company of a Spanish air force officer, and continued his journey on to Madrid under the protection of the British embassy. He stayed one night in Seville before at last arriving in Gibraltar and safety on June 23.

Having successfully evaded capture, Bob was entitled to express a preference for his next posting, and asked to be sent to Transport Command in India. He was successful in his application and also commissioned, effective from March 10, 1945. He served out the war as a navigator with 10 Ferry Unit (10 FU), flying primarily Dakotas, Beaufighters and Mosquitoes. He was awarded the Burma Star to add to his Aircrew Europe Star for operations over France and Germany.

Wireless Operator – Flight Sergeant Brian Richards – prisoner of war

Brian Ryman Richards was born on January 11, 1924, the fourth child and second son of George and Catherine. George saw service at Gallipoli, Sinai and Palestine, including a spell with the Camel Transport Corps, but died in 1930, leaving Catherine to raise the family on her own.

After schooling at the Sandgate Convent School until 1937, he attended the State Commercial High School & College (now QUT) in 1938 and 1939, but left to work as an assistant records clerk at the War Service Homes Commission. A keen sportsman, Brian was a powerful swimmer and a good tennis player, and was also known to enjoy long cycle rides with friends.

As soon as he was able, Brian joined the RAAF Reserve (two days after his 18th birthday) but had to wait until July 20 before formally enlisting and being posted to 3 ITS in Kingaroy for basic training. Selected for aircrew as a wireless operator/air gunner, Brian was posted to 3 Wireless Air Gunners School (3 WAGS) in Maryborough in September, spending several hours aloft in a CAC Wackett. Posted to 1 Bombing and Gunnery School (1 BGS) at Evans Head, Brian swapped Wacketts for the Fairey Battle, learning to shoot at drogues. With his training completed, Brian ultimately arrived at Bradfield Park and embarked from Brisbane on April 20, 1943 bound for the UK. Brian's ship travelled across the Pacific to the South American coast, then north to San Francisco. He then travelled by train to New York, visiting the famous Jack Dempsey's bar.

Arriving at Bournemouth, England on June 3, he was posted to 11 Personnel Despatch and Receiving Centre (11 PDRC was established as the receiving station for all RAAF aircrew arriving in the UK), staying at the Grand Hotel in Brighton, the hotel having been commandeered by the military for the duration. He spent two weeks with the army and a similar period with the navy, learning how the two services were structured and organised, before finally being posted to 9 AFU at RAF Llandwrog in Wales for advanced training, and thence onwards to 21 OTU where he met the rest of the crew. Brian already knew Barry by acquaintance.

On the night they were shot down, Brian made it out of the Halifax safely but was injured under the arm and suffered burns to his face and ear when his radio equipment exploded. After parachuting to the ground, he ended up in a French church near Beauvais where he was handed over to the Germans. He was given immediate treatment for his injuries at a nearby military hospital, and was briefly reunited with his air bomber en route to Dulag Luft. With Andy, Brian was sent to Stalag Luft III, and during his imprisonment promoted warrant officer.

Prior to the camp being overrun by Red Army troops, Brian was in the party forced to march to Spremberg, and then entrained for Marlag und Milag Nord, near Bremen where he suffered the same privations as their fellow Kriegies in terms of lack of food. When the camp was abandoned, the prisoners were again forced to march and their column strafed by the RAF. He was eventually liberated by the British Army and returned to the UK shortly after VE Day. His mother (as next of kin) was advised he was safe by telegram on May 11, and Brian eventually arrived back in Australia on July 28, 1945. He was discharged from the RAAF on November 2, 1945.

Flight Engineer – Sergeant 'Jack' Camp – evaded
Born on November 16, 1916, Abbott James Camp, always known as 'Jack',

was originally from Oxhey, near Watford in Hertfordshire, where his father was a landlord in a local pub. Educated at the Cave School (Harrow High School for Boys), Jack was both a grocer and a special constable before the war, and therefore in a reserved occupation. Despite this, he volunteered for military service only months after the war began.

Jack initially volunteered as groundcrew, being trained at Cardington and St Athan before qualifying as a groundcrew flight mechanic in August 1940. He spent more than six months with 107 Squadron at RAF Wattisham, then under the command of the mercurial Basil Embry, during which time he extended his knowledge of engines, being trained on the Merlin, the Tiger VIII, the Mercury, Pegasus and Wasp which powered a variety of aircraft then in service.

For two years, Jack was posted to various bombing and gunnery schools and AFUs to help service and maintain their aircraft before volunteering again, this time as aircrew, for the newly-created category of flight engineer. He returned to St Athan, and No 4 School of Technical Training (SoTT). Perhaps not surprisingly, given his experience, he qualified near the top of his class in the winter of 1943/44.

Having earned his flight engineer's brevet, and promoted sergeant, he was posted to 1658 Conversion Unit at Riccall but unusually did not join a crew. Instead, he was posted on March 16, 1944 to 466 Squadron as a 'spare'. He was by then 27, and one of the older members of the squadron. Jack flew with four different pilots during his brief time on the squadron – Pilot Officer Black (later Flight Lieutenant F B Black DFC), Flight Sergeant Sargant (later Flying Officer DFC), Flying Officer Winter (Doug Winter DFC) and Barry Casey – but only flew operations with the Casey crew. Like many flight engineers he was assiduous in keeping his log, and would include a figure to denote air miles per gallon (ampg) for each flight. On his return to the UK following his successful evasion, he completed his log for April 18 with the words: 'Operational – Tergnier. Wizard prang. Heavy opposition. Many scraps. Shot down in flames soon after leaving target by nightfighter. Baled out and escaped.'

During his absence, Jack had been commissioned and his commission was backdated to March 18, 1944. Walking into the adjutant's office, he was threatened with being improperly dressed; he was still in a sergeant's uniform but was now an officer. For the remainder of the war, Jack flew VIPs with 511 Squadron. He left the service in June 1948, with the substantive rank of flight lieutenant. For his successful evasion he was mentioned in a despatch.

One minor mystery about Jack's final flight still remains. His family remembers Jack saying that when the crew was shot down, he rendered assistance to the grievously injured mid-upper gunner, Bill Lyall, laying him on the bunk and giving him a shot of morphine. It is unlikely, however, that there would have been sufficient time. Indeed in Jack's own contemporary interview he states: 'Flames burst out and were too much to put out. We at once started to bale out.'

Escape and evasion

The following text is adapted from the official interrogation report dated January 8, 1945, upon Sergeant Camp's safe return to England. It listed his peacetime profession as 'driver and mechanic'.

'After leaving our target, the railroads at Tergnier, we took evasive action from flares, and were hit by a rocket on the port side at the rear. Flames burst out at once and were too much to put out. We at once started to bale out. It hit in a ploughed field south-west of Amiens about 2400 hours, April 18, 1944.

'One side of my harness was not fastened properly and one rib pained me badly. I buried my equipment in the hedge and looked about for other crew members. I saw none. I went by escape compass five kilometres south west and hid in a wood all the next day. The next night [I walked to] Nolléval and hid in a wood. The following morning was cold and rainy. I was given food and drink and civilian clothes in a farmhouse. From then on I walked by day and slept by night.

'I decided to make for Spain. I walked by Douville, Fleury, and the first night there went out to cut the telephone wires. Knowing I would be shot if caught, I did as much damage as possible. I walked on to Muids, Les Andelys, Gaillon and around Évreux via La Bonneville. I went on to Darnville and there I went out into the night to climb telephone poles and cut the wire.

'I next passed Bourth, Crulai, Moulicent, Nocé, Montmirail, Troo, Lavardin. At no time was I stopped or questioned. On May 1 I came to Reugny Nazelles. There was a football match going on and I attempted to steal a bicycle about 1600 hours. I was caught and the crowd nearly lynched me. I was hit on the head with a bottle and severely kicked, then tied to the back of a cart. A Frenchman asked me whether I spoke French. I said I was English. I was at once released and hidden.

'I was taken to a house for two nights and then moved to a place on May

3 where I stayed until August 18. I worked for my food and was very well treated. They tried to get me an identity card, but the stamp had to be put on in Paris and it never came back. On May 15 the Germans came into the area for manoeuvres. At night I went out and punched holes in four tanks of a petrol lorry, and threw dirt in the gas tanks of two trucks.

'On August 18 I left my friends and went with five members of the Resistance to Château-Renault. We met an MP who advised us to head for Vendôme. Near Ambloy we saw a crowd of Americans and were picked up by a unit of the Signal Corps. I gave all the information I could to a colonel there about the immediate situation around Amboise.'

'The people with whom I stayed at Nazelle from May 3 to August 18 were Monsieur and Madame Victor Vassourd. They had three children, a boy of 20 and two daughters aged 17 and 30. They lived about five kilometres from Amboise at a small place called Vallée de Vaugadeland. There is a woman in Nazelle who was an interpreter in the last war and who was a help to me. Her name is Madamoiselle Fanny Perrochon of Le Roc, Nazelles.'

Rear Gunner – Flight Sergeant Jack Swan – killed in action

Jack Edward Swan, son of Claude and Clarice, was born in Glen Iris on April 30, 1924 and educated at Melbourne High School (the school was ironically requisitioned in the Second World War for use by the Royal Australian Navy).

An intelligent young man he achieved his Intermediate in November 1940 passing examinations in maths (algebra and arithmetic), English, history, science and Latin. (He failed geometry and drawing.) Like the rest of the crew he was also a keen sportsman, and was especially accomplished at football (Australian Rules) where he gained his colours playing for the Melbourne High XVIII.

Upon leaving school he began work as a pay clerk and general office boy but seemed in a particular rush to volunteer for military service, spending three months as a gunner with the 4th Field Artillery. When he joined the reserve in December 1941, there is a suggestion that he lied about his age. Both his enrolment paper and his application for aircrew feature a wrong date of birth (December 4, 1923) that has subsequently been amended with the correct date.

Enlisting at 7 Recruitment Centre, RAAF Melbourne, Jack completed his basic training at 1 ITS (he was by now only just 18) and posted to 7 EFTS

(Western Junction) in November 1942. Initially trained as a pilot, Jack failed to make the necessary grade and master the Tiger Moth in the allotted time and, along with countless others, was remustered. Unusually, perhaps, given his academic prowess, he was not remustered as an observer but rather as an air gunner, perhaps because the training course was much shorter and it would guarantee his entry into the war more quickly. Reporting to 1 WAGS in February 1943, he passed through the course with only a minor blemish on his record: on April 30, 1943, his 19th birthday, he found himself on a charge for failing to salute a commissioned officer and was confined to barracks for seven days.

Proceeding to 3 BGS at West Sale (33 Course), his training passed without further incident and he was awarded his air gunner's brevet on June 24. Posted to 1 ED at Ascot Vale, he embarked from Melbourne on July 3, 1943 for the UK, arriving at 11 PDRC on August 12. From Brighton he was sent to Moreton-in-Marsh and 21 OTU, one of the last of the crew to arrive (on August 31). At just over five feet six and only eight and half stone, he was naturally suited to the rear turret where space was at a premium. He was promoted flight sergeant while at HCU. With his skipper and fellow air gunner, Jack Swan is buried at Poix-de-la-Somme.

Mid-Upper Gunner – Flight Sergeant Bill Lyall – killed in action

William Brian Lyall (Brian to his family, Bill to his crew) was born at Canterbury on January 21, 1921, the son of William (snr) and Hilda, when the family resided in Logan Street, Canterbury. Soon after, the family moved to Wattle Valley Road and then to Kasouka Road, Camberwell in 1927. Bill attended the Mangarra Road school in 1927, the year in which it opened as both a primary and domestic arts school.

Bill endured a difficult upbringing, his father losing his job and ultimately his house. His siblings were sent to stay with other relatives and family friends, and Bill was obliged to rely on the state to provide his school books and food. Despite such hardship, he did well at school (he gained a merit certificate from Camberwell South State School) and excelled at sport, becoming something of a health fanatic, following the latest trends in bodybuilding and diets and not averse to the odd bout in the ring.

Upon leaving school he worked as an assistant in a soft goods warehouse and as a salesman, and joined the 40th Battery, 22nd Field Regiment for three months, training to be a gunner. He applied for aircrew training the day after Pearl Harbor – December 8, 1941 – but had to wait until the following

September before reporting to I ITS. After that his training accelerated, mirroring that of his fellow air gunner Jack Swan. Like Jack, Bill was posted to 1 WAGS and then 3 BGS (Course 35), and like Jack he was successful in attaining his air gunner's brevet (August 19, 1943).

He embarked from Brisbane on September 10 and arrived in the UK on October 19 after a journey of over five weeks via the US. A month after his arrival he was posted directly to 1652 HCU and joined the crew as its mid-upper gunner. (In contrast to Jack, Bill was five feet nine and eleven and a half stone). He was also promoted flight sergeant. He is buried with Barry Casey and Jack Swan at Poix-de-la-Somme.

DIARY OF BILL LYALL

The following extracts are taken from the diary of Bill Lyall covering the period of September to October 1943. They are included to illustrate the total naivety and wonderment of many Australian servicemen of the Second World War leaving not only Australia but even their own home state for the very first time.

1943
SEPTEMBER

11th Saturday

Sailed today at 6.00 a.m. from Brisbane bound overseas, having completed exactly one year's service with the RAAF. I was enlisted in the air force on September 11, 1942, after serving 13 months in the Australian military forces. Training at Somers, Ballarat and Sale in Victoria. Graduated on August 20, 1943 as air gunner and promoted sergeant.

* Left
Melbourne
Tuesday 7th
* Arrived
Sydney
Wednesday 8th

Today is the first time I have been away from the mainland of Australia. Until Tuesday* night last, when our train crossed over the border into New South Wales, I had never left Victoria. We arrived at Sydney at 10:30 a.m., Wednesday September 8 – and moved immediately to Sydney No 2 Embarkation Depot at Bradfield Park, which is about 12 miles out of Sydney. We received leave the same night, but after being in Sydney less than an hour, we were notified to return immediately to camp. We were told that we were moving the next day and to prepare our gear.

What little I saw of Sydney in the two hours or so available, impressed me greatly. The atmosphere seemed entirely different to that of Melbourne. The mildness of the climate, the hills surrounding the city and the view of the harbour in the twilight gave me the impression that Sydney was a very fine place to live in, to stay for a few weeks or so. However, there was something else afoot for us and at 8.00 p.m. on September 9 we were on the Brisbane train. I remember on the ride into the station, on the big double decker buses, thinking as we crossed the Harbour Bridge by night [that it] must be one of the most beautiful sights anywhere in the world. The twinkling lights on the hills and rises down to the water's edge for miles around, the lighted wharves and lights reflected on the water and the illuminated ferries moving about, combined with the mild spring evening, gave me a picture of Sydney that tells me I must go back and see more of it – sometime.

We journeyed on to Brisbane, the train seeming to take its time. As it was dark, we could not notice the scenery, except when we came upon the Hawkesbury River, which was another beautiful spot by night, although I believe it is better seen by day. After travelling all night and getting what sleep was possible in the crowded compartments, we faced another full day's travelling before we reached our destination. The time dragged slowly on, as did the train, the weather was getting warmer and we were getting thirstier. This being the case, the bars on the three stations at which we stopped for meals during the day, proved very welcome.

The country was more or less virgin bush for a great deal of the way but aside from the fact that some of the gum trees were of a different type and the sight of bananas growing, not very dissimilar to Victoria in parts.

We arrived at Brisbane 7.30 p.m., Friday September 10, had our roll called and were immediately boarded on the army transports waiting some distance outside the station. We were told not to talk loudly, or attract any attention to ourselves. It was then we realised we were to go straight to the boat. After the convoy had travelled through the back streets of Brisbane, we reached the

docks, disembarked and moved onto our ship. It proved
to be the *Matsonia*, an American vessel, out before
the war, one of their crack pleasure liners. After being
allotted our quarters, we had tea and settled down for
the night. I awoke at 6.15 a.m. and realised the ship was
moving. On looking out of the portholes, I noticed we
were still in the Brisbane River, so proceeded on deck to
obtain a last look at Australia. Most of the other chaps
were there too and we stayed on deck until 7.30 when
it was time to go below for breakfast (chow in this tub).
After breakfast we were allotted various tasks to do for
the voyage – such as gun watch – which means keeping
a lookout for all things out of the ordinary. This is done
by giving each man a special section to search. Another
duty was guarding certain parts of the ship – such as
keeping personnel off prohibited areas, watching (the)
water supply to see it is not wasted etc. I was on guard
beat below so did not see much of our progress away
from Australia this morning. The chow on this ship is a
revelation. It is all American of course and pretty good
alongside some of the stuff we have had in air force
stations. Most of it is either frozen or tinned but not
bad just the same. For breakfast we had porridge with
tinned milk, tinned sausages, one hard-boiled chilled
egg and preserved loganberries. It was all very nice in
the opinion of most chaps, particularly the Yankee idea
of fruit for breakfast. There's no doubt about the Yanks –
they certainly feed their troops well compared with our
own. Another thing in the breakfast that interested me
was the fact that although the bread seemed quite fresh,
it was actually baked weeks ago in San Francisco and
was packed already sliced in airtight containers.

Our progress today has been steady and we must now
be at least 300 miles out in the Tasman Sea. It seems
hard to realise this particularly seated here in the cabin
writing this. For all the atmosphere here at the moment
I could easily imagine myself in a hotel instead of at sea.

I thought at first I may become homesick, or melancholy, being so far away from home for the first time, but on the contrary, feel immensely pleased that this long awaited trip has at last started. The day has been perfect – very few clouds – and a sparkling blue sea with our ship making a good 24 knots into the Pacific. The American soldiers on board are being repatriated back to the States for sickness and those who can walk show great interest in watching the wake of the ship as it carried them home.

We also have some US Army nurses going back – rumour has it that they are going back because of being in a certain way but we think maybe that is not likely. It is now 8.45 and I think I will turn in – the fresh air and food and prospect of this great adventure at last taking place, continue to make me both contented and tired. All the same I find myself wondering if Essendon beat Richmond in the final today and if it rained in Melbourne.

12th, 13th, 14th & 15th   Not much doing on any of these days. This transport travelling tends to become monotonous after the first day or so. Our day is filled in roughly as follows:

Rise about 7.00 a.m., breakfast at 7.30, we then clean up our cabins for the captain's inspection at 10.00. Lunch is at 11.30 and at 1.30 we go on parade to have routine orders etc. read out. Immediately after parade we are given PT which is not by any means strenuous – principally, I think, because it is not possible to have a shower afterwards. Therefore, the exercise we do get is just enough to make us breathe a little deeper. I was relieved today of guard duties and put on gun watch, on one of the AA guns, aft on the starboard side. Our watch consists of four hours on duty and 12 hours off and it is our duty to report any untoward incidents or objects in our special section. It is quite pleasant as we are going through the tropics and the sea is calm and the weather warm. Rumours are rife and the worst one says we are going to Suva, Fiji to refuel. However, I believe we have now changed course, and are heading for Auckland, New Zealand.

16th

We awoke today to find the weather very overcast. It was raining and quite cold – a definite contrast to the warm, sunny days we have been having. Around 9.00 a.m. we sighted through the rain and mist our first land for five days. We were informed that we would berth four hours after first sighting land but it was 2.00 p.m. before we sailed into Auckland harbour. This harbour is a very pretty place and somewhat similar to Sydney, although of course, not so big or busy.

We berthed at about 3.00 and at approx. 4.30 we proceeded down the gangplank on 'liberty' until 12 midnight. This was the first time I had set foot on foreign soil but it became apparent that Auckland was very little different from Melbourne, except for its size. The people seemed the same exactly and I could quite easily have imagined myself back in Collins Street or anywhere else in Melbourne. Not that I expected them to be vastly different in any way. But I did think they might have some slight accent or act slightly differently. I must say though that they were different in one respect. They are very much more hospitable (to us, anyway) than Australians.

The place was teeming with Yanks but the Aussies were definitely the fair-haired boys. About six of us, walking along the main street, deliberately set out to find out what the girls thought of us – judging by the reception our winks and grins got we were tops as far as the female population was concerned. I only wish some of the Australian girls I know, could have seen and heard the compliments we took on behalf of Australian fighting men in general, from the dozens of civilians we met that afternoon. New Zealand is very close to our own country and it was very nice to discover that Australians were thought so highly of. I think maybe those girls would have just a little bit more national pride than they have at present. Everywhere we went hospitality was showered on us. Naturally our first job being to sample New Zealand beer, we made for the nearest pub and owing (to the) insistence of the good citizens of Auckland 'filling them up' continually for the Aussies, we were looking at the world through rose-coloured glasses by the time 6.00 p.m. came round. All this for a total expenditure on our part of about 2/- each. It was certainly a great afternoon. All I can remember was that most of the time New Zealand servicemen, civvies and Maories were wanting to shake hands with us – most of the time they were buying us drinks as well.

OCTOBER
4th Monday

Owing to a fair amount of 'backsliding', I have neglected to write up this diary for approximately the past fortnight. However, as I think I can remember everything of interest during that time, I will endeavour to put it down – as far as possible, in correct sequence. Starting from the beginning – where I left off before – my stay of one night in Auckland consisted of being invited out to the home of a New Zealand digger and had a very pleasant evening, meeting his wife and three young children, plus a very nice tea followed by half a dozen excellent bottles of Auckland beer.

The evening finished with a dance to which I was accompanied by a very attractive young lady by the name of Noellene Masters, who boarded with Bert and his wife. Incidentally she is engaged to be married to an American.

After leaving New Zealand, which was about 9.00 a.m. the following day, we had a more or less uneventful trip to the USA. We crossed the International Date Line after being one day out and consequently went to bed on Friday night and woke up next morning to find it

Friday again. During the 13-day voyage the sea lived up to its name, 'Pacific', (meaning peaceful), and the weather was warm, though not unpleasantly so. After 13 days of nothing but open sea, except for two passing ships, we drew near the coast of America and awoke on Wednesday morning (September 29) to find ourselves passing small fishing boats and other craft.

After packing gear and dressing, we went on deck to watch the scene unfold, as our ship sailed down San Francisco harbour, under the Golden Gate, past Alcatraz prison and under the Oakland Bay Bridge, to a spot where we waited for a tug to pull us to our berth at the wharves.

Our first vision of America was somewhat marred, owing to a fog which hung low and obscured almost everything, even though it was around 11.00 a.m.. However, as we were destined to remain four days at 'Frisco, we were able to see the city and harbour under better circumstances. After waiting around until approx. 2.00 p.m., we eventually disembarked once more, this time on a US Army lorry which was to take us to our station for the next few days. This proved to be an island in San Francisco Bay. Angel Island, as it is named, was run by the US Army and contains a camp named Fort McDowell. It was received with mixed feelings, this new place of abode, as although it was perfectly situated as a camp, regarding condition, food and climate – the fact was the transport was not sufficient to cope with all of us RAAF personnel, as well as the US men on the island. Consequently this time we were allowed into 'Frisco only once on leave. Life on the island was more or less pleasant – the food was excellent compared to what we had served up to us during the latter part of the trip. Earlier I had said it was very good, but the fact that they overdid the bean diet, caused me to change my mind later. The first thing that struck me on entering Fort McDowell was the green trees growing in profusion all over the island. I knew there were gum trees in California but did not expect to strike them so soon. San Francisco Bay is a very attractive place – I seem to be saying that of all the places I have visited so far, but it is all new to me and I only wish I had time to think up more adjectives to describe these places. Angel Island is one of several in the bay, including Alcatraz.

On a sunny day, as it was all the time we were there, after the fog lifted, it is a beautiful picturesque spot. The warm Indian summer weather, the green foliage and the hazy blue bay, with San Francisco and the other smaller towns spread in the distance amongst the bay, make a scene that I enjoyed looking at for an hour at a time. My first visit (and only one) to San Francisco was on Friday October 1 and I must say my first sample of America was all, and more, than I expected. We arrived at the landing in 'Frisco at about 12.30, after travelling over by ferry. We found the prices a good deal dearer than in Australia – as a matter of fact, the day cost me $15.00, which is equivalent to about five pounds Australian, but then I knew this would be my only chance to see 'Frisco, so I didn't mind. I was with two of my friends, Bob and Ron, and first of all we adjourned to sample several beers at 25 cents a glass – twice as much as we pay in Australia. After the appetiser we had our first sample of American Southern Fried Chicken – very good but off went another couple of dollars.

1st

In the restaurant made our first acquaintance of American girls and had no trouble getting on friendly terms with them. Jeanne and Frances were their names – we accompanied them on a shopping tour during the afternoon and also to one or two glasses of beer.

Mixed drinking is quite the thing in the States, also the bars, which are much more elaborate than ours (and) are open until 12.00 at night. I haven't seen one drunk woman yet, or for that matter, only one or two men, so the privilege is not abused. Jeanne and Frances left us after 2.00 – had made a date with Jeanne for that night – which I am ashamed to admit I did not keep. I met another girl, by the name of Jo, who had always wanted to meet an Australian and she so fascinated me with her talk and personality, that I clean forgot about Jeanne. Jo was a university graduate and Bachelor of Science in Commercial Art and Draughtsmanship. As I had always wanted to meet the typical American college girl, I spent a very pleasant evening finding out firsthand about American universities. She had been married just six weeks and was very true to her husband, so our friendship was strictly platonic. We went to tea at a Chinese restaurant and afterwards just found a nice quiet lounge in a bar where we could have a few glasses of beer and talk. We talked until around 11.00 p.m., when I escorted Jo home to her lodgings and said good night by shaking hands. She is a very fine girl, and if she hadn't been married, and if I had been in San Francisco another two weeks I might easily have been engaged. She made me promise to write to her and if I am ever in 'Frisco again, to call on her and meet her husband. After I left Jo, I had a rather amusing experience, when I asked two girls where was a good place to eat? They just ignored my request and said: "Say that again". I did so, whereupon I was grabbed from both sides at once as they said: "Let's take him along with us – he sounds cute." So my cobber and myself went along and had supper with those girls, who were asking questions all the time about Australia. It appeared their only knowledge of Australia consisted of the fact that Australians were the best fighters in the world and that we had a song called *Waltzing Matilda*. We left these girls after having goodwill messages written on postcards etc. and promising to call on them if we ever came back there. We then adjourned to a picture theatre which went all night, to get some sleep, as we were very tired and there was no ferry back to the island until the following morning.

3rd Sunday   On this day we left Fort McDowell to travel across
                  America. We embarked for the last time from Angel
                  Island and were ferried across to Oakland, where we
                  boarded our train. Train travelling here in the States is
                  something we never dreamed of in Australia as regards
                  to comfort. After our trip from Melbourne to Brisbane –
                  with eight men crowded into one compartment – this is
                  paradise. There is a porter to every carriage and it is his
                  job to make our beds every night and morning.

                  The cars during the day are ordinary, well upholstered
                  lounges but at night, after a bit of mysterious juggling,
                  they become sleeping berths with sheets and blankets
                  and pillows. My first sleep on a train last night was as
                  comfortable as a bed at home (more or less anyway).

4th Monday   Today we awoke to find ourselves out of California and
                  in Nevada. After breakfast, which is served on cardboard
                  plates, as all the meals are on the train and they are pretty
                  good – we pulled into a small country town. Unfortunately
                  the train did not stop sufficiently long to allow us to see
                  much of it.

                  Since then we passed another town by the name of Elks,
                  which we were told by a chap who came to our window
                  to talk to us, was the 'wildest town in America' – a place
                  where they still carry guns – so he said – and that it was
                  out of bounds to all troops. He could have been kidding
                  of course. Since then we have passed countless small,
                  sprawling townships which appear suddenly out of the
                  continuous landscape of prairie, saltbush and sand as far
                  as the eye can see. These outback towns are very similar (to
                  those) I saw on the way up to Brisbane by train with very
                  little difference. At the moment we are travelling through
                  cattle country and any moment could quite imagine to see
                  cowboys in bright shirts and 45s on their hips, at one of
                  the small towns along the line. As it is the majority of the
                  citizens we have seen out here in 'the west', wear 10 gallon
                  hats. I don't think I realise yet that I am in America.

Looking out the window now it is almost possible to be looking at scenes from a western picture. This country is certainly a great place and I am looking forward to seeing a good bit more of it before we leave for England. I can see now why the Yanks are so proud of their country – they have plenty of cause to be. At the moment it is my ambition to come back here after the war – to get a college education if nothing else – and I don't think the war will change my ambition.

5th Tuesday

Still on the train and have now passed through the state of Utah. This happened late last night, hence the reason for not mentioning it before. There is not much point in writing anything of Utah as it seemed similar in all ways to Nevada. We crossed the state line from Utah into Colorado at approximately 8.00 a.m. this morning and stopped to have the train serviced at Grand Junction, about 20 miles down the line. We were allowed off the train only long enough to obtain a glass of milk and tea etc. No beer! At first we looked forward to these halts as we had visions of seeing a bit of life in a small town American community, but it is no soap as the Yank officer in charge of us watches all the troops like a hawk. Won't let us move away from the main group and insists on checking us back on the train to make sure none of us has disappeared.

Like quite a few of the Yanks in authority positions we have come in contact with since being in the States, he is very officious – you can pick the 'stay at home' joker every time. Colorado is the finest looking state we have passed though since leaving California. The scenery is very rugged – most of the way we have been travelling alongside streams and passing farmlands and orchards. Rugged bluffs tinged a reddish colour rising sheer upwards from the stream and brooks travelling along their babbling way over the rocks, give this part of the country the name 'Colorado Rocks', which no doubt the scenery does resemble – especially as there are quite a few fir trees growing on the slopes. The farmhouses, and for that matter, most of the other dwellings we are seeing now, differ quite a bit from the Australian style. In the townships the houses are vividly white with darker rooves and surrounded by green grass on all sides – that's all – no gardens to speak of and usually no fences.

The streets are wide and well shaded with trees which makes the appearance of the average street in the average American small town very attractive. I only wish I had the opportunity to stay a day or so at one of these places as I have been told that is the place to get to know the 'true American'. Although I have no complaints whatsoever regarding Americans I have met so far, they have been 'swell'.

Getting back to Colorado – from the window of a 'special troop train', it is indeed a fine looking state, – and with its warm, dry climate, thriving farms and orchards, I should imagine it would be a very pleasant spot to live. I believe it is several thousand feet above sea level. Travelling through Colorado round about dusk, I begin to understand what inspired the song, *Colorado Sunset*. There is no doubt about it, the scenery is truly magnificent.

I had a rather pleasant and amusing experience at our last stop in Colorado. It was about 9.30 and we stopped at Pueblo for about ¾ hour. We all marched to the refreshment room, and by some good stroke of fortune, they still had some beer left. I promptly ordered eight, between another chap and myself which disappeared very smartly. After knocking over this beer I wandered over to the jukebox where there were a few records playing. It was there I met Francey. It started off by me asking her if the volume could be turned up – she said it could and proceeded to do so. After a short conversation, she asked me how long we would be stopping over in Pueblo. When I told her only a few minutes, she said it was too bad as she had a car outside and if we had a few hours, she could have shown us the town. Her exact expression was: "Gee, that's too bad, my girlfriends and me would sure like to show you kids the town." However, it was too bad and I had to leave after just getting interested in her, which was a bit sad as she was very attractive.

She accompanied me out to the train and started talking to me, much to the envy of the rest of the boys in the train. After suggesting that I should make a dash away from the station and she would drive me to our next stop – a few more beers and I would have – the train blew its whistle to say we were off. Then amidst jealous catcalls and a roar of applause from the boys and much to the amusement of the people on the station, I kissed her goodbye after having made her acquaintance exactly 15 minutes earlier. Needless to say, I wasn't very much in the mood for train travelling.

6th Wednesday   Passed out of Colorado during Tuesday night and were in Kansas this morning. Weather still warm and country of the wheat farming variety. Late in the evening (about 7.00) we struck our biggest town since leaving California – Kansas City – but were not allowed, once again, to leave the train.

7th Thursday   Awoke today in Illinois after having passed through Missouri, Iowa. Approached the outskirts of Chicago round about breakfast time and ran into the station about 9.00 – we again had to be satisfied with the view from the train, which was zero.

Leaving Chicago we ran to Ohio and then to Pennsylvania. Our only stop was a few minutes at a town somewhere in Ohio, which seemed dead and didn't impress me much at all. We were let off there strictly for the purpose of exercise and were marched round the town, like of pack of sheep, for about 20 minutes. No beer – no nothing once more. About 8.00 p.m. tonight we saw our first big city by night, since we left last Sunday. It was Pittsburgh and looked very bright, although dirty, as it is an industrial town, like Chicago. The only Americans we get to talk to on most of these stops are the station gangs who service the carriages with water etc. As they are usually women it is not so bad. And so tonight finds us speeding toward New York and the end of our journey and I won't be sorry to get off this train. We have advanced our watches a total of three hours, since leaving 'Frisco, which makes us now only 15 hours behind Australian time, instead of 18. We have been informed that we get into New York about 6.00 a.m. tomorrow but do not know yet if we get leave or go straight on the boat. We are hoping hard!

466 SQUADRON RAAF
A BRIEF HISTORY

466 Squadron, Royal Australian Air Force (RAAF) was formed at Driffield in Yorkshire on October 10, 1942 and relocated to Leconfield two months later. Although intended as an all-Australian squadron, the majority of its personnel were originally British and gradually replaced as the war progressed.

Initially equipped with the twin-engined Vickers Wellington (designed by the great Sir Barnes Wallis), and forming part of 4 Group, 466 Squadron flew its first operational mission on January 13, 1943, laying mines along Germany's North Sea coast. 'Gardening', as the activity was code-named, became one of the mainstays of the squadron's activities in those first few months. Only later would it switch to its main focus, the strategic bombing of Germany.

Withdrawn from operations in the summer of 1943, the squadron re-equipped its frontline strength to the four-engined Handley Page Halifax – a lengthy conversion process that took until the end of the year to complete. The squadron did not return to operations until December 1943, and by the spring of 1944 was fully engaged in bombing targets in support of the planned invasion of Europe. In June, just three days before D-Day, 466 Squadron returned to Driffield, and spent much of July and August attacking the V1 flying bomb and V2 rocket launch and storage sites before reverting to the bombing of Germany's industrial cities and the occasional operations in support of the break out from Normandy.

By the end of 1944/start of 1945, the squadron began flying its first daylight operations, its last raid taking place just days before the German surrender – an attack on the coastal defences on the German North Sea island of Wangerooge. On May 7, the squadron was transferred to Transport Command but never fully converted to the transport role. It relocated to Bassingbourn in September and began re-equipping with the US-built Consolidated B-24

Liberator. This conversion similarly was never completed, and 466 Squadron was eventually disbanded on October 26, 1945.

According to statistics provided by the Australian archive, between December 1942 and May 1945, 466 Squadron flew 3,326 sorties against 269 separate targets. It dropped 8,804 tons of bombs and laid 442 tons of mines. In the course of these operations 81 aircraft were lost.

Squadron Motto
• Brave and true

Squadron Code
• HD

Equipment
• Vickers Wellington
• Handley Page Halifax (BIII)
• Consolidated B-24 Liberator

Battle Honours
• Fortress Europe 1940-1944
• France and Germany 1944-1945
• Ruhr 1940-1945
• Berlin 1940-1945
• German Ports 1940-1945
• Normandy 1944
• Walcheren

Casualties
• Australian only: 184 killed

Commanding Officers
• Wing Commander Reginald Edward Bailey DSO, OBE, DFC
• Wing Commander Dudley Thomas Forsyth DFC
• Wing Commander Hamilton Wesley Connolly DFC & Bar
• Wing Commander Alan Wharton DSO, OBE, DFC
• Wing Commander Albert Hollings DFC

Decorations (Australian personnel only):
• 2 DSO

- 83 DFC & 3 bars
- 2 DFM
- 1 CGM
- 1 foreign award

Histories:
• A Silverstone and S Parker, *Brave and true: A history of 466 RAAF Halifax Squadron whilst based in Yorkshire England as part of Four Group, Royal Air Force* (Sydney, 466-462 Squadron Association, 1992)

466 SQUADRON OPERATIONS RECORD MARCH–APRIL 1944

Adapted from the 466 Squadron Operations Record Book and relevant combat reports, with additional commentary by Sean Feast. The period covers the six weeks the crew spent on the squadron.

March 1/2
Bombing Attack on Stuttgart
Sixteen aircraft ordered, five failed to take off due to engine trouble and ice on wings. Six returned early – one with R/T, heating and guns unserviceable, two with hydraulic trouble, one with the ASI unserviceable, one with icing on wings and one with engine trouble (landed at Ford). All six jettisoned bombs. Remaining five attacked target and returned safely, two of them landing away from base. Total bombs dropped on primary 160 x 30lb incendiaries, 3,300 x 4lb incendiaries and 300 x 4lb 'x' type incendiaries. Should be a good attack if the fires were in the town as they could be seen from a great distance away. Very few fighters seen on target or en route.

March 6/7
Bombing attack on Trappes
Thirteen aircraft were detailed, all became airborne and attacked and returned safely. Total bombs dropped on primary target: 103 x 1,000MC TD 0.025 plus 90 MC TD 0.0251. Bombing was good and not scattered. One heavy flak gun reported but believed knocked out early in attack. No searchlights or fighters anywhere.

March 7/8
Bombing attack on Le Mans
Thirteen aircraft detailed and became airborne. Nine aircraft successfully bombed primary target but remaining four failed to identify target and jettisoned loads in sea as instructed at briefing. Total bombs dropped on primary target: 65 x 1,000lb MC TD 0.025 and 69 x 500lb MC TD 0.025. One aircraft descended to 5,500ft and got below cloud but was unable to

see ground detail. He reports bombing rather scattered. Three crews report a large explosion at 21.59 hours. Four fighters seen over target, none en route. A little light flak and no searchlights.

March 15/16
Bombing attack on Stuttgart
Eighteen aircraft were ordered and 17 took off to attack target; one returned early owing to illness and jettisoned bombs in the sea (Flying Officer Bernard MacDermott was captain of aircraft). Fourteen aircraft attacked primary target and one jettisoned live 20 miles from the target. One aircraft missing, one aircraft ditched in the sea on return – navigator missing. Eight others landed away from base. Total bombs dropped on primary: 6,720 x 4lb incendiaries, 840 x 4lb 'x' type incendiaries; plus 672 x 30lb incendiaries. The aircraft bombed on red ground markers which are reported as scattered. Only a few fires seen in the built-up area. Green/red sky markers were five miles north of ground markers and incendiary fires could be seen there. The raid was not all concentrated. Fighter activity confined to the target area.

Pilot Officer William Russell and his crew had to endure three separate attacks from nightfighters in which the rear gunner (Flight Sergeant Douglas Quarti) was wounded, but not before he and the mid-upper gunner (Flight Sergeant William Cashman) had claimed their own unidentified twin-engined aircraft as probably destroyed. Their aircraft returned with a gaping hole in the port main plane, and countless smaller holes peppered the fuselage. (Bill Russell was killed the following month as a flying officer DFC. His Distinguished Flying Cross, and a Distinguished Flying Medal awarded to Flight Sergeant Cashman for their actions on March 15/16, appeared in a supplement to the *London Gazette* dated April 25, 1944.)

Another Halifax, skippered by Flight Sergeant John Bond was attacked and damaged on the run in to the target and its fuel tanks holed. Short of petrol, Bond was obliged to ditch in the sea, 30 miles south of Portland Bill. All of the crew emerged unharmed with the exception of the navigator, Flying Officer Oswald Chrimes whose body has never been found.

Of another of the crews there was no news, although the Red Cross would later report that Pilot Officer Harold Wills and his crew were safe, having originally been reported missing. It was later learned that their aircraft had been severely damaged by a nightfighter and the oxygen cylinders set on fire. With the threat of imminent explosion, Wills just had time to hold the aircraft straight and level long enough for he and the crew to escape by parachute, a feat that may have earned the pilot higher praise. As it was, his reward was several burns to his hands and face, although he lived to survive the war as a POW.

(In 1945, Wills was debriefed on his return to safety: "About 100 miles on home run aircraft attacked by fighter from starboard beam which scored hits immediately in the centre section behind the engineer's panel and in overload petrol tank. Aircraft burning furiously and on pulling out of evasive action at 18,000/17,000ft ordered abandon. No acknowledgement received as had to remove helmet and mask because of burns received. On replacing same the intercom was dead. Remained circling until approx 4,000ft then baled out. Aircraft in fair control until baling out then commenced spin and crashed on edge of Hagenan Forest. Aircraft was on fire all the way down and exploded on contact. All crew successfully baled out and have now returned to the UK. Wireless operator/air gunner (WAG) evaded capture and returned home via Switzerland. No injuries apart from self. Landed on hill overlooking small village about one quarter of a mile away. About one and a half hours later made my way down to village and entered police headquarters. Identified as RAAF officer and handed over to Luftwaffe. Transferred to Prison Hospital Strasbourg for treatment and then prison camps. Released by Russians 1/5/45.")

Arguably the luckiest crew of the night was the one skippered by Flight Sergeant F C Pope. They were attacked twice: once on the way in, and once again on the way home. The first attack was forewarned by 'Monica' – an early warning radar device designed for the very purpose of detecting an enemy aircraft before it attacked. Monica's alarm, however, coincided with the first fiery beads of tracer arching towards the bomber from astern, but fortunately passing wide. The gunners did not have time to return fire before the fighter – identified as a Junkers 88 – subsequently disappeared. The second interception came almost exactly an hour later, and this time Monica gave the gunners more warning. Another Ju88 was attempting to creep up on them from astern without being seen, but was spotted by Flight Sergeant Hewett in the rear turret who called for evasive action and opened fire, as did the mid-upper Flight Sergeant Dalton. No hits were claimed on the fighter but the bomber sustained slight damage to the fuselage. It could have been much worse, and it was a very tired and very relieved crew that crawled into their beds that morning.

March 18/19

Bombing attack on Frankfurt

Twelve aircraft detailed and airborne. Two returned early due to hydraulic trouble and jettisoned loads in sea. Seven aircraft bombed primary target and returned safely. Three failed to return and have been reported missing. Total bombs dropped on primary: 4,620 x 4lb incendiary bombs, 420 x 4lb 'x' type incendiaries plus 392 x 30lb incendiaries. The markers were fairly well concentrated and the area was covered with incendiaries which lit up the sky. Several fighters seen but aircraft of this squadron had no combats. Moderate heavy flak at target; searchlights very active on way out.

The three crew lost were those of 21-year-old Flight Sergeant John Richards RAAF, from Cottesloe, Western Australia; Pilot Officer Malcolm Watson RAAF, a 30-year-old from Casino, New South Wales; and 22-year-old Flight Lieutenant Lancelot ('Lance') Curnow RAAF. Watson, who was on his sixth operational sortie, was one of three brothers, all of whom were aircrew in the RAAF, and all of whom were killed during the war. One had been killed in a collision whilst at OTU; another on his first operation with 460 Squadron. Curnow had joined the RAAF in June 1940 and arrived at Leconfield in July 1943. He was one of the squadron's most experienced pilots.

Richards' aircraft was reportedly shot down by flak. Curnow may well have been the victim of a nightfighter flown by a novice pilot of I/NJG6. Only four out of the 21 men in the three aircraft survived to become prisoners of war.

Warrant Officer Robert Bray, the air bomber with the Richards' crew (Halifax HX231), was one who survived to become a prisoner of war. He later reported: "The aircraft was hit by gun fire from an unknown source. My intercom was shot away so no orders were received by me except by visual signals from the wireless op (Wop – Warrant Officer George De Fraine). Navigator (Flight Sergeant Kenneth Wilson) left by front escape hatch some minutes before me. I baled out next from 19,000 feet. Aircraft under control. No fire observed, but due to lack of oxygen was not a competent observer of such facts. Wop still in aircraft when I left. Lying in snow and picked up by German Home Guard. Later made contact with navigator and engineer (Flight engineer – Sergeant D F Wooldridge). Germans said four of the crew had been killed. Thigh and stomach muscles torn and spent time in hospital then in prison camps. Liberated by British Army on April, 15, 1945."

Subsequent enquiries after the war and investigations by a missing research and enquiry unit reported that the aircraft of Flight Lieutenant Curnow (Halifax ZW369) crashed near Pfungstadt on March 18, 1944 presumably as a result of enemy action. Pfungstadt is approximately five miles south west of Darmstadt, Germany. Six of the crew were killed and they are buried in the Durnbach War Cemetery. Durnbach is a village ten miles east of Bad Tolz, a town 30 miles south of Munich.

The rear gunner in the Curnow crew, Sergeant Forrester (RAF), who survived to become a POW later reported: "The Germans told me that five of the crew got out and one body was in the aircraft. They gave me the names of all of them with the exception of PO Taylor (the navigator). So he must have been the one left in the aircraft. The rest got out but their chutes did not open apparently. I was told by a German doctor that I could see where they were buried but was moved before I could walk. Resting place about four miles west of Darmstadt."

March 22/23
Minelaying in Kiel harbour
Ten aircraft were detailed and took off, one returned early. Nine aircraft laid mines successfully and returned safely. Flight Sergeant Ross Robertson and crew were abortive, having had problems with the electrical circuit. They returned with the mines still on board. Total mines dropped: 18 x 1,500lb mines.

Bombing attack on Frankfurt
Three aircraft were detailed and one was later cancelled. Two aircraft became airborne and one returned early owing to being off track – the compass suspected of being unserviceable. The remaining aircraft attacked the target and returned safely. Total bombs dropped on target: 660 x 4lb incendiaries, 60 x 4lb incendiaries 'x' type plus 56 x 30lb incendiaries. Markers were good and as aircraft left target the incendiary fires were beginning to take hold and smoke was rising. Moderate heavy flak at target and only one fighter seen.

March 24/25
Bombing attack on Berlin
Fourteen aircraft were ordered and became airborne. Two returned early (one unable to gain height; one with Gee unserviceable – the latter being the aircraft of the squadron commander). One aircraft jettisoned bombs 60/70 miles south of the target, one reported missing. Remaining 10 aircraft attacked primary target and returned safely, two of them landing away from

base. Total bombs dropped on primary: 4,890 x 4lb incendiaries, 600 x 4lb 'x' type incendiaries plus 480 x 30lb incendiaries. Widespread incendiary fires were reported and red glow of fires were seen for over 100 miles on returning. One big explosion in target area. Defences were moderate. Fighters active from Flensburg area to Magdeburg. All aircraft returned south of track owing to incorrect broadcast winds.

The missing 466 Squadron Halifax (LV900) was flown by 20-year-old Flight Sergeant Ross Robertson. He was thought to have been a victim of a nightfighter.

March 26/27
Bombing attack on Essen
Sixteen aircraft were ordered, 15 took off – one non-starter. Fourteen aircraft attacked primary target and returned safely. One returned early owing to short circuit in rear gunner's electrical suit and jettisoned bombs in the sea. Total bombs dropped on primary: 7,620 x 4lb incendiaries, 840 x 4lb 'x' incendiaries plus 864 x 30lb incendiaries. Aircraft bombed on the glow of the red and green markers. The bombing was fairly concentrated but no results could be observed. Defences at target were very moderate, searchlights practically nil. Fighters were active from target to coast on return. Route was fairly quiet on the whole.

Flight Sergeant Ronald Walsh and his aircraft were attacked within minutes of releasing their bombs. Sergeant H N Lloyd, the mid-upper gunner, spotted the twin-engine nightfighter while it was still some 500-yards distant and called for a corkscrew. The pilot put the Halifax into a diving turn to starboard and the nightfighter was lost. (Walsh's luck eventually ran out in July when he was killed).

Another of our NCO pilots was also attacked whilst leaving the target area. Flight Sergeant C R Wilson (later Flying Officer DFC) had just completed his bombing run when his mid-upper gunner, Flight Sergeant R J Poggs, identified a Focke Wulf Fw190 about to attack from 600 yards. The gunner shouted "corkscrew starboard" and simultaneously opened fire. The fighter also opened fire and closed to within about 300 yards before breaking off his attack. Neither aircraft was hit and both disappeared into the night.

Halifax LV875 flown by Flight Sergeant John Cole (later Flying Officer DFC) was also attacked and lucky to come away unscathed. The gunners did not see the fighter until it opened fire but luckily from too great a range for it missed. The mid-upper gunner (Flight Sergeant Milner) returned fire but the rear gunner (Flight Sergeant Close) could do nothing as his turret would not rotate. He could only watch as a spectator as the pilot corkscrewed to avoid further attacks.

March 30/31
Bombing attack on Nuremberg
Seventeen aircraft were ordered, 16 took off – one a non-starter. Twelve aircraft attacked primary target and returned safely. One aircraft returned early owing to complete cut of starboard inner engine; another owing to the illness of the navigator; a third owing to u/s heating system; and the fourth due to lack of oxygen to the rear gunner (causing him to pass out. This was the aircraft of a flight commander who would later go on to command the squadron, Squadron Leader Hamilton 'Pat' Connolly DFC, who had arrived in the UK in 1941 and was one of the first Australians to fly the Halifax). Bombs in respect of these jettisoned safe. Total bombs dropped on primary: 6,390 x 4lb incendiaries of which 640 were 'x' type; plus 600 x 30lb incendiaries. Owing to cloud it is not ascertained if PFF were concentrated but bombing was very scattered and it would appear that Schweinfurt area received a larger proportion of the attack. Fighters were active from Aachen to Stuttgart. A number of aircraft landed away at Odiham, Lasham, Lindholme and West Malling.

This was the night that Bomber Command suffered its greatest losses. Remarkably, not a single 466 Squadron aircraft was lost, and only one appears to have suffered damage through enemy action. This was the Halifax of Pilot Officer William Russell (LV875), whose rear gunner (Flight Sergeant Cashman) was once again engaged in combat with an enemy fighter, a Bf 109. Cashman did not call for evasive action until he was certain the fighter was committed to the attack, at which point he called for a corkscrew and opened fire. Hits were seen to strike the fighter from both the rear and mid-upper turrets. They claimed the fighter as probably destroyed.

April 9/10
Bombing attack on Villeneuve-Saint-Georges
Fifteen aircraft were ordered and all became airborne, attacked the target and returned safely, one landing away from base. Total bombs dropped on target 83 x 1,000lb MC TD 0.025 plus 134 x 500lb MC TD 0.025. Several crews reported that the railway tracks of the marshalling yard were

seen in the light of the bomb flashes. Four aircraft reported a large orange explosion at 24.00 hours in the target area. Two other aircraft saw two large red explosions at 00.03 hours in the target area.

April 10/11
Bombing attack on Tergnier
Fifteen aircraft were ordered and all became airborne. Thirteen attacked the target and returned safely; two missing. Total bombs dropped on target: 74 x 1,000lb MC TD 0.025 plus 109 x 500lb MC TD 0.025. Five aircraft achieved aiming point photographs. One crew reported hits on marshalling yards – flak was slight; no searchlights. Considerable fighter activity on leg out from target. Several unidentified aircraft were seen to go down in flames. (Ten bombers were lost on the Tergnier raid.)

The first of the two missing aircraft (Halifax HX274) was captained by Flying Officer Colin Lamb. Lamb, from Hawthorn, was 25 and had enlisted in the RAAF in 1940. The only survivor of the crew, the navigator Flying Officer Slatter, was liberated from a prisoner-of-war camp by the Soviets in May 1945. His report confirms that they were a victim of a nightfighter attack: "Aircraft shot down over target near St Quentin Northern France. 'All out, give me my chute Wop' ordered the captain. Not acknowledged. Don't know if any injured. Aircraft was out of control. Don't think on fire. I baled out at 10,000ft. I was unconscious. Last I saw of crew was in the aircraft but don't think any escaped. Germans said they were all killed and that the aircraft attempted a crash-landing but exploded 100 feet off the deck." Their victor was Unteroffizier Leopold Weinberger of 7/NJG4 for his second 'kill'. (Weinberger was himself killed two weeks later in an accident caused by engine failure.)

There were no survivors from the second crew lost that night, that of 23-year-old Flight Sergeant John Bond. Their aircraft (Halifax LV875) was shot down by Leutnant Joseph Springer of 8/NJG4. Bond, from New South Wales, had endured a short but highly eventful operational career, having survived a ditching the previous month.

April 19
Bombing attack on Tergnier
Fifteen aircraft were ordered and took off to attack target. Fourteen aircraft attacked the target and returned safely, one landing away from base. One aircraft reported missing. Total bombs dropped on primary target: 72 x

1,000lb MC TD 0.025 plus 105 x 500lb MC TD 0.025 plus 22 x 500lb LD. PFF markers were in two clumps, one definitely to the west of the aiming point. The master bomber directed aircraft to bomb those to starboard, but not all aircraft heard him. A fair weight of bombs must have fallen on target. Defences were slight: several aircraft reported to be seen shot down on way home. (Six bombers were lost on this raid.)

In a 1945 statement the then Warrant Officer Brian Richards, Wop within the crew of Flight Sergeant Barry Casey, reported: "Aircraft was hit by flak in the bomb bay. The intercom and electrical system were destroyed. Aircraft began to burn immediately. No order to bale out because intercom was unserviceable. Assumed later that both gunners (Jack Swan and Bill Lyall) were killed by flak. The navigator (Bob Wallace), bomb aimer (Andy Wiseman) and engineer (flight engineer Jack Camp) went before me. The pilot and two gunners were still in the aircraft when I left at approximately 4,000ft. Aircraft was in a steep dive and all but the nose burning fiercely. Aircraft crashed near Beauvais. Landed in field and captured next morning. Met bomb aimer after capture. Germans said three killed in aircraft. Navigator and engineer escaped to the UK. Released by British Army 30/4/45."

SOURCES

Public Records/archives

NAA: A9301, 420638	Service record of Barry William Casey
NAA: A705, 166/7/474	Casualty record of Barry William Casey
NAA: A9301, 419661	Service record of William Brian Lyall
NAA: A705, 166/25/135	Casualty record of William Brian Lyall
NAA: A9301, 419234	Service record of Jack Edward Swan
NAA: A9300, Wallace J R	Service record of John Robert Wallace
IS9/WEA/8/156/1281	Evasion report of Temp/Sergeant A J Camp
AIR/27/1926	Operations Record Book 466 Squadron RAAF
AIR/50/268	Combat Report – Halifax LK793
	Combat Report – Halifax HX243
	Combat Report – Halifax LV900
	Combat Report – Halifax HX274
Intelligence Summaries	Luckenwalde April–May 1945
Night Raid Report No 581	Night operations April 18/19, 1944
5 Group Tactical Notes	(2nd edition November 1943)

Private Records

Logbook of Jack Camp

SELECT BIBLIOGRAPHY

466 Squadron RAAF Second World War Fatalities
Alan Storr (Australian War Memorial, 2005)

*Against the Sun: The Story of Wing
Commander Roland Beamont DSO OBE DFC*
Edward Lanchbery (Cassell, 1955)

Accident – the Death of General Sikorski
David Irving (Willam Kimber, 1967)

Footprints on the Sands of Time
Oliver Clutton-Brock (Grub Street, 2003)

Handley Page Halifax: From Hell to Victory and Beyond
K A Merrick (Classic Publications, 2009)

Royal Air Force Bomber Command Losses (Volumes 5, 7 and 8)
W R Chorley (Midland Publishing, 1997, 2002, 2003)

Stalag Luft III: The Secret Story
Arthur Durand (Louisiana State University Press, 1999)

Tales of My Time
Raymond Baxter with Tony Dron (Grub Street, 2005)

The Halifax at War Brian Rapier (Ian Allan Publishing, 1987)

The Last of the 39-ers
Sean Feast (Grub Street, 2013)

We act with one accord
Alan Cooper (J & KH Publishing, 1998)

PERSONAL THANKS FROM SEAN FEAST

This book could not have been written, of course, without the close co-operation of its subject, Andy, and what genuine fun and a privilege it has been. I learned a great deal about things that I had never come across before, especially regarding his postwar career, and I hope that I may even have taught Andy something along the way as well.

The list of individuals to thank starts with Derek Camp, son of the flight engineer in Andy's crew. Derek provided invaluable help in sourcing the service records of Barry Casey and his fellow RAAF aircrew, as well as some most excellent photographs. David Champion was similarly a vital link in providing much background and detailed information about Andy's time at Luckenwalde, including intelligence summaries for April and May 1945.

Alan Dobson, the former BBC editor par excellence, provided a number of wonderful anecdotes to complement Andy's own memories, and Neil Galloway MBE was also a great help in updating me (and reminding Andy) of the various events and reunions that he had been instrumental in arranging. Thank you gentlemen.

Of fellow writers and enthusiasts I'd like to acknowledge the help of another Grub Street author Oliver Clutton-Brock for his unrivalled knowledge of all-things POW, Jason Warr, and John Dann from the Friends of 466/462 Squadron Association (Halifaxlv827.co.uk).

As ever, I am always grateful for the support of my PR colleagues Iona, Alex and Imogen for making my 'real' job so interesting and a constant challenge, and to the fantastic team at Grub Street for producing such a stunning array of fascinating books that continue to adorn my shelves. Finally, to my genius wife and boys Matt and James who ensure (not always intentionally) that no one day is ever the same!

INDEX